On Your Bike
Derbyshire &
Nottinghamshire

❀

Tim Hughes and Jo Cleary

COUNTRYSIDE BOOKS
NEWBURY, BERKSHIRE

COUNTRYSIDE BOOKS
3 Catherine Road
Newbury, Berkshire

To view our complete range of books,
please visit us at
www.countrysidebooks.co.uk

ISBN 1 85306 732 6

Designed by Graham Whiteman
Maps and photographs by the authors

Produced through MRM Associates Ltd., Reading
Printed in Italy

CONTENTS

AREA MAP SHOWING THE LOCATIONS OF THE RIDES

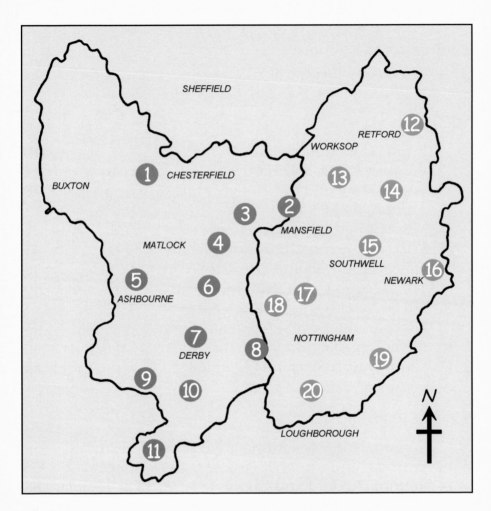

Route

1 Eyam, the Plague village
2 Bolsover Castle and Hardwick Hall
3 Beeley Moor and Cat Hole
4 Around Matlock
5 Tissington Trail and Ilam
6 Wirksworth and Carsington Water
7 Hole-in-the-Wall and Osmaston Park
8 The Erewash Valley, Nutbrook Trail and Dale Abbey
9 North of the Dove
10 Melbourne, Repton and Calke Abbey

11 South-west Derbyshire
12 Retford, North Leverton Mill and Clayworth
13 Worksop and Clumber Park
14 Retford, Tuxford and Laxton
15 Southwell's countryside
16 Newark's northern villages
17 Lord Byron Country
18 On the trail of D H Lawrence
19 The Vale of Belvoir
20 Nottinghamshire Wolds

INTRODUCTION

From the beginnings of recreational cycling, when the bicycle endowed ordinary people with the means of travelling much further afield than they could on foot, the Derbyshire hills became a weekend 'lung' for the inhabitants of the industrial towns and cities nearby. More people reside in towns and cities surrounding what is now the Peak National Park – Britain's first – than live in Greater London. And it seems particularly fitting to encourage people to explore the lanes of Nottinghamshire by bike since the city of Nottingham has become synonymous with their manufacture. As far back as the 1880s Thomas Humber of Beeston, west of Nottingham, was renowned as one of England's finest makers of quality bicycles and tricycles and today the Nottingham cycle makers, Raleigh, are world famous.

Between them, Derbyshire and Nottinghamshire provide rich samples of England's inland landscape, from the rugged uplands of the northern Peak District to the fenlands of north Nottinghamshire. Though some of the rural parts seem untouched – Laxton in Nottinghamshire is the last place in Britain to practise medieval strip farming – the Industrial Revolution has left deep scars on both counties, particularly where they meet. The prosperity of the area grew with the rise of the coal industry and to some extent fell with it. A feature of the colliery villages was the looming hill of the spoil tip, made up from unwanted rock extracted at the same time as the valuable coal. With the closing of the pits, there has been a concerted effort to stabilise and grass over these mounds and plant them with trees as open spaces for general recreation. The more established have become wildflower meadows and havens for wildlife – such as skylarks, the numbers of which had declined as a result of intensive cultivation. This new landscape is freely accessible and you can cycle on the paths where these are firm-based. Some of the scars left by former mineral railways are also healing and the tracks left behind are finding a new life as trails for cyclists, riders and walkers.

All this means that though our routes seek out quiet country lanes, from time to time you will be reminded of the area's industrial heritage, which is no bad thing and certainly worth the odd half-mile of cycling between stern rows of colliery houses. In other places you will meet the remnants of the once-great

Sherwood Forest and towns and villages with sometimes unexpected literary and historical associations.

Cycling remains the best way to travel. It's not just what you can *see* from a bike, it's also what you can hear, feel and smell. Beanfields and pine forests smell the same when you're in a car, a skylark is a dot in the sky but on a bike you can enjoy the different scents and can hear the birdsong high above. Cycling lets you deploy these four senses to the full – and at the end of the ride you can enjoy deploying the fifth, as you tuck into your well-earned meal and savour your chosen drink.

Our routes are all about gentle, enjoyable cycling – and spread over a leisurely day, you can easily cover the distances of these routes, on any kind of bike. Most of the routes are in gentle country, too, but we've put in a few more challenging ones in the distinctly up-and-down part of Derbyshire. Here the rewards are the exhilaration of being in upland country and the swoop back down to the valley at the end! And it's not a race so if a hill seems a bit steep, there's no shame in walking. If you feel a bit hungry or thirsty, stop for something to eat or drink and if you see something intriguing, pause to take a look. The whole point is enjoyment and the fun of exploration and discovery.

Tim Hughes and Jo Cleary

GUIDE TO USING THIS BOOK

Each route is preceded by details to help you:

The **number of miles** under the title is the total for the ride; some rides have possible short cuts turning them into two (or more) shorter routes. Most of the routes are on roads with hard surfaces but several use short lengths of easily ridable firm track or path – as useful links to avoid a main road, say. One or two use longer stretches to see the best of the area, particularly those that go through forests, or where the alternative roads are unattractive.

The area map of Derbyshire and Nottinghamshire shows where the twenty routes are. They have been arranged as if you were reading north-to-south down the two counties: they are *not* in order of length or difficulty. Each route is accompanied by a simple **sketch map**, intended to give you a general idea of where the routes go but best used in conjunction with an Ordnance Survey map (see below).

The brief **introduction** to the ride gives a broad picture of the route and what you can see along it.

The information box gives details of useful maps, the exact location of the starting point, refreshment places and the hilliness or any other possible difficulties along the route.

The maps listed are all Ordnance Survey sheets in the Landranger 1: 50 000 series. You could probably follow the route from our description and sketch map but it is advisable to take the Landranger map with you as a back-up – and to tell you what that 'interesting-looking place over there' is.

The starting point is a particular point in a village or town including its Ordnance Survey map grid reference. For starting points reachable by public transport we mention the other places served. Most of the starting points have car parks nearby though we cannot guarantee that you can always park free of charge.

Possibilities for refreshment, such as pubs or tearooms, are mentioned in the information box and others may be named in the text for the ride. (Don't overdo the liquid part of a pub lunch: it is against the law – as well as very foolish – to ride a cycle under the influence of drink or drugs.) Because a picnic can be the most enjoyable cycling lunch on a fine day we also mention shops where you can buy food.

Parts of the Derbyshire rides that go into the Peak National Park are really hilly, but some indication about ups and downs appears with all of the routes. The box also warns of any stretches of main road to be negotiated in case you are interested in the route's suitability for children.

THE ROUTES
It is a good idea to read right through a route before setting out so that you know what's involved and can note any places where you may want to spend more time. The routes are roughly circular and each starts and ends in the same place but obviously you could start and finish wherever you want – or go round in either direction. It's easiest to follow instructions in the order they're given, though. As far as possible, rides start from places you can reach by public transport.

The directions have been written as clearly and briefly as possible. Instructions to change direction are printed in bold type: **Turn R** at the T-junction, or **bear L** at the church. Instructions to continue straight on are not in bold.

The directions include some 'tourist information', but after the route description there is more information about selected **places of interest**.

SAFETY AND COMFORT
Make sure that your bike and those of any companions – especially children – are roadworthy and that they are adjusted to fit their riders. There are quite a number of good books on bikes and their maintenance but if you are not confident enough to do it yourself get the bikes checked by a proper bike shop. Make sure that everything that should be tightened *is* tightened and, most importantly, that brakes and gears are working properly. Also make sure any beginners and children in the party know how to use them.

If your bike starts out in good condition most mishaps will be no more than minor, the commonest being the dreaded puncture. Even here you can help avoid trouble by not riding over obviously sharp things such as broken glass, and keeping a look out for debris from roadside hedges that have recently been cut. If necessary walk round or even carry your bike over the worst thorny bits. The best way to be prepared to deal with punctures is to carry at least one, preferably two, spare inner tubes of the right size and just replace the punctured tube – after checking the inside of the outer tyre and removing the sharp object that caused the hole in the first place. This will mean slipping the wheel out and then back in (which may need spanners if you haven't got 'quick-release' wheel hubs), and getting the tyre off (which will need levers) and on again (which shouldn't). It's worth getting somebody to teach you the drill before you go. And it's essential to make sure you or at least one person has a decent pump with the appropriate connector(s) to fit all the party's bikes.

If you are not riding alone, make sure that the pace suits everyone or that you arrange that those who are ahead will stop every so often to give the others time to catch up. Some people may not be as fit, as practised or – yet – as fond of cycling as you are. Don't put them off or make them feel they're holding the group up: look after them – especially children, who will certainly ride at a slower pace and need more stops.

You are likely to get quite thirsty, and possibly hungry, while riding, so it's worth having a water bottle and some odd bits of carbohydrate food such as biscuits or bananas with you. Neat water bottles fit into the bottle 'cages' fitted to many modern bikes.

Carry things securely, preferably in proper bike bags, not on your back, and make sure you don't have things dangling off handlebars, panniers or clothing. A rogue 'bungee' elastic strap can be deadly! A bike lock is useful for peace of mind if you're going into a pub, teashop or place of interest. Remember to remove valuables such as wallets, cameras and mobile phones from bags when you leave the bike unattended, and if you can, lock the bike to something immovable.

Wear comfortable clothes – with as few seams as possible in the saddle area: special padded cycling shorts, which can be worn as undergarments in cooler weather, make a tremendous difference. Shoes should be comfortable, too, with firm soles. For the top half, several layers of thin clothing, so that you can adjust to differing terrain and temperature, are better than one or two thick ones. And because cycling

moves you through the air faster than walking you may still need gloves on warmer days.

A helmet does offer some head protection if you fall off. If you buy one, choose one that conforms at least to the current British Standard (BS6863), or to the more stringent requirements of the American Snell Institute. Whether a child's or an adult's make sure that it is the right size, properly secured and properly worn.

If you are going to be out after dark, or even if there's a chance you might not get back before dusk, make sure you have adequate front and rear lights and that your bike is fitted with a rear reflector. Be wary on unlit or patchily lit roads, particularly if the road surface is poor: probably most after-dark cycle accidents are caused by riders hitting unseen potholes, road defects or debris.

Use common sense. Ride sensibly and obey road signs and traffic lights, particularly at junctions with busier roads. Don't try to do things such as reading maps or guides or reaching for things in bags while riding unless you're very practised at it.

Eyam: The Plague Village

12 miles

This first route is our shortest but is an ideal introduction to the range of scenery you can find in the Peak Park. River valley, open upland grazing, moorland and some fine stretches of woodland – this ride has them all. The main historical attraction is the village of Eyam and its tale of heroism from the 1660s.

Maps: OS Landranger 110 Sheffield and Huddersfield and 119 Buxton, Matlock and Dove Dale. Only the first 2 miles out and the last mile back are on sheet 110 and it would be possible to manage on sheet 119 alone. The route comes onto sheet 119 at GR 202800 and leaves it at GR 233800 at the top edge of the map.

Starting point: Hathersage Station (GR 233810); there are ramps down to road level from both platforms. Trains from Sheffield, Stockport and Manchester call at Hathersage (not all trains stop here) and there are some special services at weekends for walkers and cyclists coming into the Peak Park. Hathersage is about 9 miles south-west of the centre of Sheffield. There is a public pay-and-display car park in the village itself.

Short cuts: You can't really shorten the route without missing Eyam – and it's already quite short.

Refreshments: There are plenty of pubs, shops and tearooms in Hathersage which like all Peak Park villages tends to get crowded at summer weekends. Otherwise there are pubs offering food in Leadmill (on the B6001 just after crossing the River Derwent), Great Hucklow (just off the route), Foolow and Eyam, which also has a tearoom and small shops.

The route: The terrain is very hilly in places, both up and down; some of the downhills call for caution. There is no main road to be negotiated on this route.

From Hathersage Station exit, **turn L** to the B6001, and then **turn L** on the B-road (no signs). Go over the River Derwent and almost immediately after the bridge, towards the brow of a slight slope and opposite the Plough Inn, **turn R**, signposted 'Abney' and separately to the Gliding Club.

The little road climbs quite steadily to become a shelf road with views, first to the right over the River Derwent and the Hope Valley and then to the left over the steep valleys (or 'cloughs' as they are

Bretton Clough, near Abney

known) of the Highlow and Bretton Brooks. The road runs through a mixture of woodland and open fields to the hamlet of Abney, where there is a sharp dip to cross the Abney Brook and then a climb away from it. The next mile or so is through a landscape of stone walls then, after Abney Grange which is on the left, the

road climbs steadily again to the wooded slopes of Hucklow Edge.

At a very oblique T-junction, **turn very sharp R** (no signpost) and downhill to the outskirts of Great Hucklow. Just before the village sign for Great Hucklow, **turn L** on a very minor road, signposted 'Grindlow'. (If you want to visit the

11

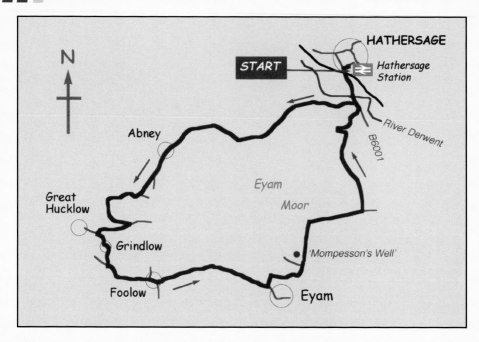

village – or its pub – go straight on and then retrace to this junction.)

After going through the hamlet of Grindlow, just a huddle of grey stone cottages, there is another T-junction, once again unsignposted. **Turn L** to reach Foolow, with its cross on the green, and keep round to the **L** past the Bull's Head, signposted 'Eyam, Grindleford'.

After about 2 miles you come to the outskirts of Eyam; the turning you need to leave the village to continue the route is to the **L** soon after you come into the village, Hawkhill Road, signposted 'Youth Hostel', and just before a small general store. The main part of Eyam, including the church and its record of the Plague is about ¼ mile straight ahead; to continue the

route after visiting it, retrace to this junction.

The climb out of the village is quite steep, with what is almost a little gorge through a wooded avenue partway up. At the end of the woodland, continue straight on, signposted 'Grindleford', to pass Mompesson's Well, one of the Plague landmarks. The road continues to climb quite earnestly up to the open heather and bracken moorland ridge of Eyam Moor.

The road bears round to the right and starts to go steadily downhill and as the slope steepens, and just before the 'steep hill 10%' warning notice, **turn L** (no signpost). This road is a pleasant wooded avenue, with heathland to the left, later dropping steeply to a couple of very sharp bends, the first to the left, the second to the right. Views open up over the Derwent valley to the right, and the road drops to join the B6001. **Turn L** on the B6001 (no signpost) to pass the Plough Inn and cross back over the Derwent towards Hathersage. Just after passing under the railway arch, **turn R** into Station Approach (signposted 'Station') and back to Hathersage Station.

• •

GREAT HUCKLOW

This village, a few yards off our route, was a centre of leadmining up to the end of the 19th century. There is evidence that extraction of the ore began as early as the 11th century, with further evidence of a settlement here from Iron Age times.

EYAM AND THE PLAGUE

The serious outbreak of bubonic plague in 1665–1666 – unlike the Black Death or Great Pestilence three centuries earlier – affected mainly large cities and the south of the country. However, it threatened to reach out into north-east Derbyshire in the autumn of 1665 when – according to tradition – a roll of what proved to be infected cloth from London arrived at the workshop of a tailor in Eyam. It had become damp on its journey and when it was laid out to dry, plague-infected fleas escaped. The unfortunate tailor died within days and more and more contacts succumbed. The rector of Eyam, Rev William Mompesson, saw the danger in the spread of the disease and persuaded the inhabitants to cut themselves off from contact with the outside world. For over a year food and medical supplies were left at agreed points on the boundary of the village, and the coins to pay for them were left in running water, disinfected with vinegar. One of the exchange points, 'Mompesson's Well', lies a few yards off our route. By October 1666, when the Plague ended, 259 of the village's 350 inhabitants had died – but the surrounding villages and towns had been spared. Many of the buildings in the village which have survived from those times carry plaques detailing the sad but heroic story. Interestingly, Eyam had been one of the first villages to have a piped water supply when about a dozen stone troughs were built in 1588 with drinking water piped from springs.

Although the Plague features prominently in the Eyam Museum, the village museum also covers a wider history of village life. Eyam Hall, too, is worth a visit.

Bolsover Castle and Hardwick Hall

18 miles

The settings for the two great houses along this route could hardly be more different. Bolsover Castle looks out over a former coalmining valley and a 19th-century planned village for its miners, whereas Hardwick Hall (or Halls, really, because there are two), only 4 miles away, is set in a great park with magnificent trees and land grazed by rare breeds of sheep and cattle.

Map: OS Landranger 120 Mansfield and Worksop.

Starting point: Langwith-Whaley Thorns Station is on the Robin Hood Line from Nottingham to Worksop (GR 529708). The former mining village of Whaley Thorns is about 7 miles north of Mansfield and some 6½ miles south-west of Worksop. There is a small station car park.

Short cuts: It wouldn't be easy to shorten the route appreciably without missing out either Bolsover Castle or Hardwick Hall – which rather defeats the object.

Refreshments: There is a wide choice of cafés, restaurants and pubs in Bolsover, including the tearoom at the Castle Visitor Centre; there is also a tearoom at Hardwick Hall but you have to pay to get into the grounds to reach it. There are pubs in Whaley, Glapwell, Langwith Junction and Nether Langwith, and village shops in Glapwell and Nether Langwith.

The route: The terrain is fairly gentle except for the climb up through Hardwick Hall Park. As with several of our routes, you actually go *down* a couple of the steepest hills on the circuit. The route is entirely on-road (apart from the 600 yds of track on the alternative return to Langwith-Whaley Thorns station). There are three short sections of A-road: the A632 in Bolsover itself, the A617 after Rowthorne (only 200 yds but rather busy with an alternative pavement if you'd rather walk), and the ½ mile of A632 in Langwith, which doesn't even look like a main road.

Go up the ramps from the platforms at Langwith-Whaley Thorns station and **turn L** down the path through the car park to a mini-roundabout. **Turn L** on North Street and after about 200 yds take the **second R** on a narrow road opposite a sign for 'The Woodlands'; follow this past Whaley Thorns Primary School to a T-junction. (If you miss the narrow turning, don't worry: The Woodlands loops round and brings you back to the right road.) **Turn L**

Hardwick Hall

and follow this road, mainly uphill, for about ½ mile to a T-junction.

Here, **turn L** on a road marked with a 5-ton limit. About ½ mile later there is a level crossing; the gates are normally shut but there are pedestrian wicket gates to the left of the main ones. Go through (look out for trains!) and continue for about 700 yds to a road fork with a white-trimmed stone cottage (unnamed) in the angle. **Bear L** – do not follow the road markings – to a T-junction by the Black Horse in Whaley village. **Turn R**, signposted 'Bolsover', past a red telephone box. The road climbs steadily for nearly 2 miles to a

crossroads with the B6417. Go straight over (unsigned – *ignore* the 'Bolsover' signing left along the B6417).

On the outskirts of Bolsover **turn L** by a school to a mini-roundabout junction with the A632, with the parish church prominent ahead. Go straight on up the slope and, just past the church at the top, **turn acutely R** into High Street, with a brown sign to the Castle. After about 400 yds follow the road round to the right: it becomes Castle Street and there is a steep (16%!) lane, Castle Lane, to the left with a remarkable view, and a small viewpoint a few yards down

15

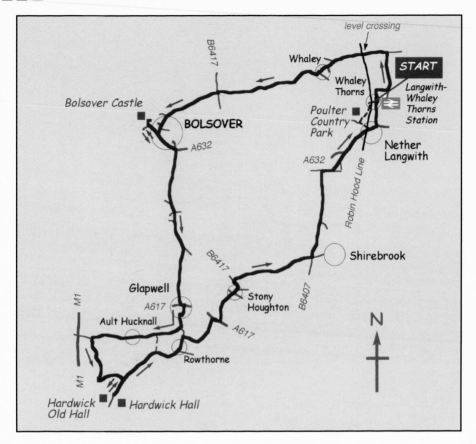

it. The entrance to Bolsover Castle is about 200 yds further along Castle Street (not down the hill), on the left, with a Visitor Centre housing a tearoom.

Retrace the outgoing route back along High Street to the junction with the A632. **Turn R** and continue for about ¼ mile and, at the start of Hills Town, **turn R** into Mansfield Road, signposted 'Palterton, Glapwell'. This road has broad views over the Trent valley to the left and glimpses of the steeper valley of the Doe Lea to the right with the

Derbyshire Peak hills beyond. At a fork after nearly 2 miles, **bear R**, signposted 'Glapwell' and in Glapwell itself go straight across the A617 into Rowthorne Lane.

Just beyond the end of the village **turn R**, signposted 'Ault Hucknall, Stainsby'. There are very good, if distant, views of Bolsover Castle on its crag to the right just before and after the hamlet of Ault Hucknall. The lane drops steeply and with bends and at the foot of the hill, just after a small bridge, **turn L** to follow a brown sign to 'Hardwick

Hall'. This is a fine sweeping climb, first through farmland and then winding through the open woodland (or wooded meadowland) of the park. There are two or three cattle grids across the road: the easiest way to tackle these is to ride straight over them at normal speed – the faster the better (not always easy uphill!). Take care if they are wet; otherwise they are much easier to ride across than to walk over. The road round to the Halls (there are actually two) sweeps round to the right.

To leave the park, retrace the outgoing route for about 300 yds as far as a sign which says 'No entry or exit' at the top of the hill you rode up. Take great care over this section as you are travelling against the motor traffic one-way flow. **Bear R** at the 'No entry or exit' sign (which applies to car traffic) and follow this wide oak-flanked avenue to the lodge gates. Go through the wicket gate to the side of the main gates and continue to a forked junction. **Bear R**, signposted 'Rowthorne'.

At the far end of the attractive stone-built village of Rowthorne, **turn R** on a narrow road which is unsignposted, opposite a cast-iron lamp post. The road sweeps round to the left to meet the A617. **Turn R**, unsignposted, for about 200 yds, and then take the **first L**, signposted 'Stony Houghton'. This section of the A617 does carry quite heavy traffic at times – it's

one of the main links from the M1 to Mansfield. If you don't feel like riding along it, you can walk the 200 yds or so along the pavement on the far (north) side of the road.

In the hamlet of Stony Houghton (which isn't signed) you come out on a double bend on the B6417. Go straight on the B6417 for about 50 yds, then **turn L** after Hall Farm past a red telephone box. After several bends and a short ride uphill **turn R**, signposted 'Shirebrook'. There are broad views ahead towards the forest of Clumber Park and then the road drops to a crossroads on the outskirts of Shirebrook. **Turn L**, signposted 'Langwith', and continue for about 1½ miles to a T-junction by the Devonshire Arms. **Turn R** (unsignposted) past yet another red telephone box to reach an oblique junction where you have to give way to traffic coming in from the right. Continue straight on along the A632 to pass under a railway bridge, with traffic light controls, on the outskirts of Nether Langwith.

There are *two choices* of route here, one involving a short section off-road. For the *road route* continue straight on for about 200 yds, then **turn L** into Pit Hill, over a small bridge, and signposted 'Whaley Thorns Heritage Centre' and also signed to the station. Pit Hill becomes Bathurst Terrace, and at the end of the terrace, **turn L** at the mini-roundabout to go through the car park to Langwith-Whaley Thorns Station.

For the *off-road route*, **turn L** immediately after the railway bridge with the traffic lights, signposted 'Archaeological Way' with a car park sign. This goes immediately under another high railway bridge and passes a small lake to the left. About 300 yds further on, by the remains of another railway bridge, **turn R** into the car park for Poulter Country Park. Go straight across the car park and then round to the left of the stone wall barrier at the end of the car park, then straight ahead across what might eventually be an extension to it, to join a firm-based gravel track. Follow this track over the shoulder of the hill straight down to Langwith-Whaley Thorns Station. The total length of the off-road section is about 600 yds.

BOLSOVER CASTLE

Bolsover Castle on its crag dominates the valley of the River Doe Lea much as Hardwick Hall does. But Bolsover Castle seems all the more surprising, even if it is a mere 5 miles away, because it looks out over an industrial and former colliery landscape, to say nothing of the M1 and the poor Doe Lea, at one time stigmatised as the most polluted river in Britain. Although there was a Norman motte-and-bailey on the site, the current Bolsover Castle dates from the 17th century peak of the English Renaissance, and features elaborately carved fireplaces, richly painted rooms and elegant courtyards. There is a Hardwick

connection here, too: it was largely built by William Cavendish, grandson of Hardwick's Bess. For opening times and admission charges etc phone 01246 241569 or visit www.english/heritage. org.uk.

WELL DRESSING

Although well dressing – decorating wells with usually religious pictures made from flower petals and other natural elements pressed into wet clay – is more generally associated with villages such as Tissington in the Peak District, the three Derbyshire villages of Ault Hucknall, Rowthorne and Glapwell, all on the route, have their own ceremonies in mid-July each year. A Derbyshire Well Dressings leaflet is available (telephone 01246 242324).

HARDWICK HALL

Hardwick Hall is much the more famous of the two great historic houses on this route. In fact there are two halls at Hardwick – Hardwick Old Hall, now in the care of English Heritage, and Hardwick Hall, owned by the National Trust. Both were built by 'Bess of Hardwick' (Elizabeth, Countess of Shrewsbury), said to be the richest woman in England after the Queen, Elizabeth I, thanks to her practice of serially marrying rich noblemen destined to predecease her. The Old Hall is now ruined but retains its commanding views over the park and towards the new hall behind it. The New Hall houses famed collections of furniture, tapestries, needlework and paintings. For opening times, admission charges etc for the New Hall phone 01246 850430 or visit www.ukindex.co.uk/nationaltrust, and for the Old Hall 01246 850431 or www.english/heritage.org.uk. Access to the fine 500-acre wooded park which is home to rare breeds of sheep and cattle is free to cyclists during daylight hours.

Beeley Moor and Cat Hole

21 miles

Beeley Moor is the largest stretch of open upland country on any of our routes and gives a wonderful feeling of broad horizons and tall skies. This is in utter contrast to the intimate valleys, domestic fieldscapes and the man-made lake that make up the eastern half of this exhilarating ride.

Map: OS Landranger 119 Buxton, Matlock and Dove Dale.

Starting point: Ogston Reservoir car park (GR 376610). This is the one just off the B6014, approximately 2 miles south-west of Clay Cross; there are toilets (not open all the time) and picnic tables.

Short cuts: It would be possible to shorten the route but it would mean missing out Beeley Moor, one of the highlights of the trip.

Refreshments: There is a tearoom/restaurant at Scotland Nurseries (about 4 miles after the start; see route description). Although it wasn't designed that way, this mainly upland route is remarkably pub-free. Actually on the route there is the New Napoleon at Fletcherhill, just after the start, then none until the Bull's Head at Holymoorside, the only other one. Just off the route is the Manor House Inn, about ¼ mile down a lane which leads off to the right, part way down Bole Hill, about 4½ miles from the end of the trip. There is a village shop in Holymoorside – and that's it.

The route: The terrain is hilly to very hilly, although there are some longish near-level stretches along ridges and a glorious 3-mile descent to Holymoorside. Apart from two crossings of the not very busy A632 there is no main road to be negotiated on this route.

From the exit from Ogston Reservoir car park **turn L** opposite Hill Cottage on the B6014 to cross the head of Ogston Reservoir. Just past the stretch of road with water on both sides, **turn L**, signposted 'Woolley, Brackenfield'. This road follows the edge of the reservoir through the hamlet of Woolley to climb slightly to Brackenfield. At Brackenfield church, follow the road round to the right, signposted 'Tansley, Matlock', and continue uphill past the broad open space of Brackenfield Green (on the left), and ignoring all turnings to the left.

After about ½ mile the road curves round to the right. Just past a large house on the left, **turn L** into Coldharbour Lane (no other direction signpost). This lane is a fairly short but steep climb; however, there's the consolation that once you're up you stay up for quite some distance – and there's a view of Ogston Reservoir back over your right shoulder. Ignore a fork on the right which goes steeply downhill and continue past an 'official' viewpoint on the right to a T-junction with the B6014. **Turn L,** signposted 'Tansley, Beeley', over the brow of the hill to a minor slightly staggered crossroads. **Turn R,** signposted 'Kelstedge', (Scotland Nurseries with a useful coffee shop and restaurant is about a 200-yd detour further on along the B6014).

Once you are clear of the trees there is a view over to the left of the folly of Riber Castle (which features on Route 4). After about ¾ mile the road comes to a point where another comes in from the right and an unsurfaced track goes straight ahead. **Bear round to the L** and continue for about 1½ miles to a T-junction with the A632; **turn L** uphill, signposted 'Matlock' and then almost immediately **R,** signposted 'Beeley, Darley Dale'.

Follow this road – which runs alongside woodland for some way – for about 1¾ miles and take the **first L turn** at an oblique minor crossroads, where all the directions except the one you want are signed! After about ¾ mile, **bear R** at a T-junction, signposted 'Darley

Dale, Stone Edge', to reach a crossroads with the B5057. Go straight over into Flash Lane, signposted 'Beeley Moor', and continue for about 1½ miles to a T-junction with a slightly more significant road than the one you've been following. Go straight over (no signs) onto a wide and firm-based but untarred track – mind the potholes and puddles!

When this track meets a tarred road, after about ½ mile, **turn L** (no signs) on the road, which leads to the open heather moorland of Beeley Moor. Once over a slight brow there is a fine view ahead across the Derbyshire hills. The road begins to go gently downhill but don't get carried away: after about ½ mile take the **first turning on the R,** which doubles back across the moor. After about another ½ mile, go straight over at a minor crossroads (no signs) into an attractive and exhilarating minor road down a valley known as Cat Hole to the village of Holymoorside.

In Holymoorside, take the **first R,** just before the Bull's Head, signposted 'Walton', up quite a steep climb out of the village, Cotton Mill Hill. Just after what looks like the top of the hill, take the **first R** turning, Bage Hill (no direction signpost), to continue the climbing theme to the real top. After just under a mile you reach the A632; go straight over into High Lane which climbs to a T-

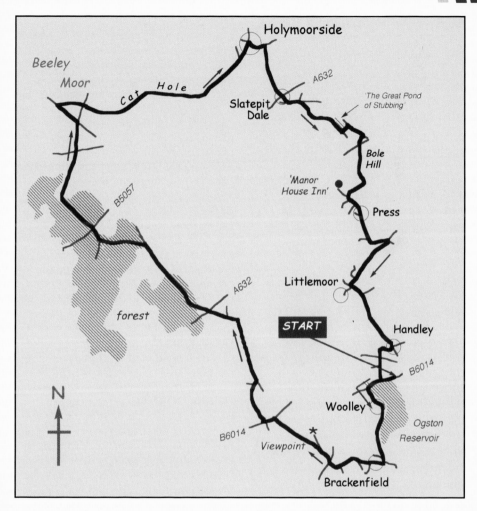

junction, where you **turn L** (no signpost). The road goes slightly downhill and after about ¼ mile take the **first R**, Steep Lane – which it is: down, fortunately.

At the bottom of the hill, **turn L** into Malthouse Lane, with the stately pile of Stubbing Court to the right and a small reservoir on the left, apparently called The Great Pond of Stubbing. At the foot of the Pond, **turn L** across the dam, signposted 'Wingerworth', and at the far end, **turn R**, signposted 'Tupton, Clay Cross'. After about ½ mile, **turn R** at a T-junction, signposted 'Ashover, Darley Dale', then after a short climb, take the **first L**, signposted 'Alton', to go over Bole Hill. It's a stiff climb up, but a fine winding descent the other side.

Ignore all turnings right off this road and you will eventually find that you are following signs for 'Clay Cross'. Just after crossing a bridge over a little stream there is a T-junction with a minor road. **Turn L**, again signed 'Clay Cross', to follow the stream valley for about ½ mile to another T-junction; **turn L**, signposted 'Tupton, Clay Cross'. Another ½ mile, another T-junction; this time **turn R**, signposted 'Littlemoor, Ashover', continuing for about a mile uphill to a crossroads on the outskirts of Littlemoor.

Turn L, signposted 'Handley, Stretton', and then after about ¼ mile, take the **first R**, Woodhead Lane, signposted 'Handley'. This road is a bit of a reward for the climbing: slightly downhill, then contouring with fine views to either side. In the hamlet of Handley **turn R** at the crossroads, signposted 'Woolley Moor, Ogston', and follow the winding descent to the next crossroads with the B6036 by a church. Go straight over, signposted 'Ogston, Woolley', **bearing L** at the next road fork and down to the B6014 with the waters of Ogston Reservoir directly ahead. **Turn L** by the New Napoleon, signposted 'Clay Cross, Tibshelf', back to the Ogston Reservoir car park.

OGSTON RESERVOIR

The reservoir was created in 1958 when the River Amber was dammed and over 200 acres of the valley flooded. As with many artificial lakes, with maturity Ogston Reservoir has become a haven for birds and over 200 species have been recorded here; there are two observation hides. Facilities include picnic areas and public toilets. There are fine broad views over the water from several points along our route and from the picnic areas.

BEELEY MOOR

Beeley Moor is unlike anything on any of our other routes: a wide open upland spread of mostly heather-covered moorland. In late August it is a brilliant purple carpet that gradually shades into russet as autumn advances. At any season it is an inspiring place to be, with a tremendous sense of openness to the changing sky. It is a haven for ground-nesting birds though very boggy in places.

HOLYMOORSIDE

Holymoorside, at the foot of the exhilarating descent of Cat Hole from Beeley Moor, is now mainly a dormitory village for people working in nearby Chesterfield or even Sheffield, but in the past it had an industry of its own. In the last half of the 19th century it boasted a prosperous three-storey cotton thread mill, but trade waned and it closed in 1902. Now only the names of Cotton Mill Hill and Dye Mill Yard remain as reminders. For followers of our route, however, Holymoorside is more likely to be welcomed, and remembered, as almost the first chance for refreshment since setting out on the route.

4

Around Matlock

19 miles

The deep valley of the River Derwent which cuts into the limestone uplands of the White Peak means that this is quite a hilly route, so take it steadily. The rewards are some attractive stone villages and wooded steep-sided valleys. There's history here, too: you could say the Industrial Revolution began with Richard Arkwright's water-powered cotton mills at Cromford.

Map: OS Landranger 119 Buxton, Matlock and Dove Dale.

Starting point: Matlock Station (GR 296603). The car park at the station is for rail passengers only, but there is a public pay-and-display car park just to the north of it. Trains from Derby run to Matlock, the end of the line on this now-truncated route which used to offer a superb run through the Peak Park to Manchester. There are ambitious – but inevitably long-term – suggestions of re-opening the whole line. A short section of it carries on about 4 miles up the valley through Darley as the preserved Peak Railway. It would also be possible to start and finish the route at Cromford Station (GR 303574).

Short cuts: It would be difficult to shorten the route significantly without cutting out one or more of the points of interest.

Refreshments: There are plenty of pubs, shops and tearooms in Matlock. Otherwise there are pubs offering food in Wensley (the Red Lion boasts home-baked brown cobs), Winster, Bonsall, Cromford, Holloway, and Lea. There is a small café at the Crich Memorial Tower (closed Wednesdays) and a teashop in Lea, the Coach House (closed Mondays).

The route: The terrain is very hilly in places, both up and down; some of the downhills call for caution. Apart from two very short stretches of the A6 at the start and finish there is very little main road to be negotiated on this route: about 1 mile of the Via Gellia into Cromford and 600 yds of the A615 near the end.

From Matlock Station exit, **bear R** through the station car park to the A6 by the bridge over the River Derwent. **Turn R** on the A6 and immediately **keep R** (effectively straight on where the A6 goes left) by a rather ornate classical-temple false entrance to the Royal Bank of Scotland. This is Snitterton Road, though it's not named at this junction. Continue up (and we mean up, for about ¼ mile) this time past the real entrance to the Royal Bank. Across to the right

23

Some of the attractive architecture in Winster

there are glimpses of the broadening view over the Derwent valley, then the road drops slightly and goes round a right-hand hairpin bend through the hamlet of Snitterton.

The road climbs again, more gently, past another hamlet, Oker, up the right-hand side of a small valley to a T-junction with the B5057. **Turn L**, up a steep little pitch to the pretty stone village of Wensley, then more gently to the more substantial settlement of Winster – also an attractive village with its National Trust Market House.

At the far end of the village and just before a bend to the right, **turn L** by the Dower House into West Bank, which climbs quite steeply up to an oblique junction with the B5056 by the Miner's Standard. **Turn L**, signposted 'Ashbourne', for about ¼ mile. **Turn L** on a minor road, Bonsall Lane, signposted 'Bonsall Moor'. There are several remains of mine buildings near the road, which climbs quite gently to the highest point on the route – about 1,135 feet – with some fine views ahead and to the left.

The road then begins to go steadily downhill at a nice freewheeling slope with no need to grab at the brakes through the few farm buildings of Brightgate. About ½ mile further on the road narrows quite significantly and swoops downhill through the village of Bonsall. **Bear R** just in front of the antique village cross on its plinth, past the King's Head to the left. At the foot of the village follow the road round to the left, signposted 'Cromford, Matlock', down a 1-in-6 hill (about 16%) to a T-junction with the A5012, the so-called 'Via Gellia'. The 'Via Gellia' is *not* a Roman road but was named after himself by a Mr Gell, a 19th-century quarry owner.

Turn L, signposted 'Cromford, Matlock'. After about a mile – downhill – the road comes into Cromford. At a T-junction opposite Arkwright Stores, **turn L**,

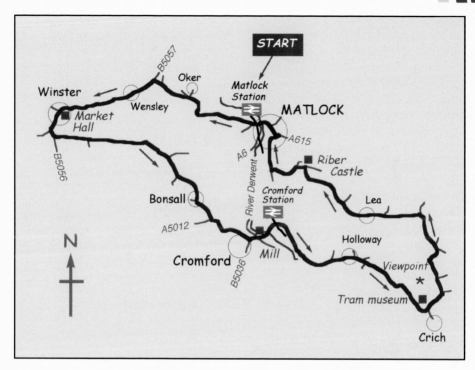

signposted 'Derby, Matlock' to the junction with the A6, controlled by traffic lights. **Go diagonally R**, across the A6, signposted 'Lea, Holloway, Crich', into Mill Lane (or Mill Road), which soon passes the refurbished mills. Follow the brown tourist signs for the 'Tramway Museum', over the River Derwent and then **R**, signposted 'Lea, Holloway, Crich', into Lea Road and under the railway bridge by Cromford Station.

The road follows the river for about a mile then bears round to the left to Lea Bridge. **Turn R**, signposted 'Holloway, Crich', and start climbing again, quite steeply, up to Holloway. Go straight on, following

signs for 'Crich', and the road levels out – or at least climbs more gently – with views off to the right. In Crich, the road bears round to the left past the entrance to the National Tramway Museum and just after this **keep round to the L** where the major road goes right into the main part of the village, into Plaistow Green Road, signposted 'Moorwood Moor, Tansley, Memorial Tower'.

After about 200 yds, at a right-hand bend in the road, a track leads off to the left to the Tower, where you will find a snack bar, toilets and fine views all round. Be warned though: getting in will cost you, as a cyclist, 10p! And it's closed on

Wednesdays. To continue, the road goes gently downhill, then **bears sharp L**, signposted 'Tansley, Wheatcroft'; carry along on this road for about 2 miles, following signs to 'Tansley, Matlock'. At a T-junction with High Lane, **turn L**, signposted 'Lea, Holloway'; after a short distance the road name changes to Lea Moor Road.

This straight road reaches the village of Lea after about a mile and, shortly after passing the Coach House restaurant and tearooms on the right, **turn R** into Bakers Lane at a minor crossroads (no signpost), to go steeply downhill for about 200 yds to a T-junction. **Turn R** (no signpost) to go steadily uphill for about a mile to a T-junction, where you **turn L**, signposted 'Riber village'. After about ¼ mile you come to another T-junction by a triangular green; **turn L** (no signpost) to continue on the route, or right to Riber Castle and the Wildlife Park.

Shortly after turning left you go down a winding 1-in-5 hill (20%), which is regularly used (in the opposite direction!) for cycling hill-climbs. After the very steep section finishes the road comes to a T-junction in Starkholmes; **turn R** (no signpost or road name at this point). This goes downhill to the A615 opposite the Horseshoe, where you **turn L**, signposted

'Matlock' (although you're really already in it), to a mini-roundabout junction with the A6. **Turn L** over the river bridge and immediately after the bridge **turn R** into Matlock Station entrance.

• •

WINSTER MARKET HALL

This fine example of an old stone-built market hall stands in the middle of the main street of the village. The lower authentic arches are thought to be about 500 years old, but the upper portion was restored, using the original materials, in 1905. It was the first local property to be acquired by the National Trust, as long ago as 1906. It now houses a National Trust information room. Winster also boasts its own website, www.winster.org.uk, which gives more information on the village's history and attractions.

CRICH TRAMWAY MUSEUM

In the rather unlikely situation of a worked-out quarry just outside Crich village, high above the Derwent valley, is the National Tramway Museum. The Museum houses, in addition to trams – which are in operation – other vintage public transport and features reconstructions of early 20th-century streets and shops contemporary with the tramway exhibits. Days and times of opening vary with the season: it is open every day from April to the end of October, but for winter opening times telephone 01773 852565. There is a charge for admission which includes all exhibits and unlimited tram rides. There is also a restaurant. By the way, it's pronounced 'Cryche'.

5

The Tissington Trail and Ilam

17 or 9 miles

The railways' loss is the cyclists' and walkers' gain, with this traffic-free trail which climbs steadily into the heart of the Peak, one of the most popular recreational routes in the country. Tissington and Ilam, the two main villages on the route, are both estate villages but very different. Tissington is the best-known of the Derbyshire villages that have 'well dressing' ceremonies, when the village's wells are blessed and decorated. There's an unexpected delight towards the end of the longer route with the great grassy parklands of Blore and Okeover.

Map: OS Landranger 119 Buxton, Matlock and Dove Dale.

Starting point: Mapleton Lane car park, about ½ mile west of the centre of Ashbourne (GR 174469); this is a pay-and-display car park. On the same site are toilets, a cycle-hire centre, shop and light refreshments. The nearest rail station is Tutbury and Hatton (see Route 9) but this is 12 rather hilly miles by minor roads to the south of Ashbourne. Uttoxeter on the same line offers a less hilly but longer (14-mile) B-road route.

Short cuts: The route may be shortened to about 9 miles by following the trail only as far as Tissington, taking the Thorpe road out of the village and returning via Mapleton.

Refreshments: There are only two pubs actually on the route, at Hopedale, about halfway round, and Mapleton, only 1½ miles before the end. There is of course plenty of choice in Ashbourne. Light refreshments are available at the start, at the Hall in Tissington, and in Milldale, where Polly's Cottage is a sort of teashop off-licence, selling refreshments at the door to be eaten out in the open. But if the weather's anywhere near decent this is really picnic country, with many choices of attractive stopping places as well as many seats and picnic tables; stock up in Ashbourne before you set off and stop when you feel like it.

The route: This is a route of two halves. On the Trail, which has a hard crushed-stone surface, the terrain is mostly a gentle climb, while once off it the road section is quite hilly, with a particularly tough climb up from Ilam to Blore. Apart from a crossing of the relatively minor A515 after the Alsop en le Dale car park there is no main road to be negotiated on this route.

On the Tissington Trail in winter

From the start, follow the Trail northwards, following direction signs for 'Tissington'. Soon after the start, the route goes through a gate, down a steep slope and up another the other side on the site of a missing former railway bridge. A sign advises cyclists to dismount – which you may want to do for the short distance as it's a bit bumpy. From here the Trail climbs gently: in fact its whole trend in this direction is uphill, almost imperceptibly for the most part, since gradients on railways had to be quite shallow. Nevertheless the Trail climbs from 425 ft or so above sea level at the start to about 886 ft at the point where you leave it, and one restored railway gradient sign shows it to be as steep as 1-in-20 (5%) at one point. There are occasional distance markers, seats and picnic tables along the route.

After about 3½ miles the route reaches Tissington, where there are again trailside facilities such as toilets and a picnic area. It's worth leaving the Trail for a few hundred yards here to look at the attractive village of Tissington – besides, there's a tearoom at the Hall.

From the Tissington 'service area' follow the signs up the Trail to 'Alsop', which is 3 miles further on. This stretch of the Trail is a mixture

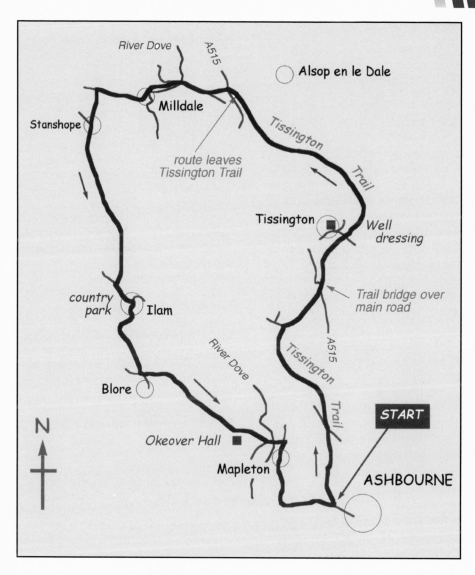

of cuttings and embankments, and broad views begin to open up. At the Alsop car park (more picnic tables) **bear L** off the Trail, across the car park to the main A515, and straight over onto a minor road, signposted 'Milldale, Alstonefield'. This road goes quite steeply downhill to an oblique T-junction, where you **bear R**, still downhill and again signposted 'Milldale, Alstonefield'. Immediately after the picturesque bridge over the River Dove, **fork L** on a minor road, signposted 'Milldale', to follow the river down to the village of

29

Milldale itself, at the head of Dove Dale.

By the bridge follow the road round to the **R** to begin to climb steadily up a steep-sided grassy valley to the cluster of houses and a pub which form the hamlet of Hopedale. Just after the pub, **turn L**, signposted 'Ilam, Dove Dale', to go up quite a steep little pitch for about 100 yds, then **first L**, still signposted 'Ilam, Dove Dale'. This is an up-and-down road between stone walls, reaching 303 metres (tantalisingly inches below the 1,000 ft mark) at its highest point before swooping down to the village of Ilam where you follow the road round to the L.

At a triangular green with a monument in the village keep round to the **R**, effectively straight on and signed 'Blore', to cross the bridge over the River Manifold. The road climbs quite steeply through open grazing grassland and, after the gradient eases, past an attractive picnic area, 'Blore Pastures'. At a minor crossroads just before the hamlet of Blore, **turn L**, signposted 'Mapleton' (although it's 'Mappleton' on some maps) and 'Ashbourne'.

This road is a lovely long swoop down to the Dove valley, past the entrance to Okeover Hall. Just after the bridge over the River Dove the road climbs to a T-junction in Mapleton, where you **turn R**, signposted 'Ashbourne'. This road

contours round the flank of the river valley for about 1½ miles back to the starting point just outside Ashbourne.

● ●

THE TISSINGTON TRAIL

The Tissington Trail is one of a trio of old railway lines in west Derbyshire and east Staffordshire that have been converted into firm-based paths for cyclists and walkers (the other two are the High Peak Trail, which it joins, and the separate Manifold Valley Trail to the west). It follows part of the route of the old LNWR Ashbourne to Buxton Line, which opened in 1899 and closed in 1967, and now has a fairly smooth ash and gravel surface, though it does tend to get a bit dusty in very dry weather.

WELL DRESSING AT TISSINGTON

Tissington is probably best known for its well dressing ceremonies when, around Ascension Day, the village's wells are decorated with tableaux of biblical scenes. A Derbyshire Well Dressings leaflet is available (telephone 01246 242324).

ILAM

Ilam is one of those villages that was displaced when the squire wanted to enlarge his manor. In the first half of the 19th century, the new owner of the village built a new Hall, renovated the church and moved the whole village further away to its present position. The Hall and its grounds now belong to the National Trust; the Hall itself has been a youth hostel for over half a century and is not otherwise open to the public. The grounds, however, – a fine mix of open parkland and woods – are open free of charge.

Wirksworth and Carsington Water

19 miles

There's no denying that, like the route from Matlock, this is a hilly route, but at least you get the toughest climb out of the way just after the start. The viewpoint at Alport Heights gives one of the broadest views in the southern part of the Peak, and there's a special treat later in the designated cycle path round part of man-made Carsington Water. Quite a number of our other routes go through former coalmining areas; the mining on this ride goes back even earlier, to Roman times when leadmining began near Wirksworth.

Map: OS Landranger 119 Buxton, Matlock and Dove Dale.

Starting point: Ambergate Station (GR 349516); there is some car parking nearby. Trains from Derby to Matlock and vice versa stop at Ambergate, which is about 11 miles north of Derby.

Short cuts: It would be difficult to shorten the route significantly without cutting out one of its highlights, the path round Carsington Water.

Refreshments: There are pubs in Ambergate, Belper Lane End, Kirk Ireton, Hopton, Wirksworth, Wirksworth Moor (the Malt Shovel) and the Bear Inn on the way back to Ambergate. There are teashops in Ambergate, a small kiosk (seasonal and weekends) at the south end of Carsington Water, a larger café at the Water Visitor Centre and teashops in Wirksworth. There is a small shop at Ambergate (on the A6 just beyond the point where the route turns off the main road) and a very small shop-cum-post office in Kirk Ireton; otherwise the only ones we saw were in Wirksworth.

The route: This is a very hilly route, with some steep pitches both up and down. Apart from the few yards of the A610 and A6 at the start and finish there is no main road to be negotiated on this ride.

Leave Ambergate Station by the access road to the car park, and **turn L** on the main road (no signpost) to go under the railway bridge to the A6. **Turn L** on the A6 opposite the Hurt Arms, signposted 'Belper, Duffield, Derwent Valley Visitor Centre, Derby'. Just after Ambergate Cricket Ground on the right, **turn R** into Holly Lane, signposted 'Youth Hostel'. The road crosses the River Derwent and then bears round to the left and rears very steeply uphill. Don't be put off if you have to walk: this road is regularly used for cycling hill-climb championships!

Carsington Water

After about 300 yds, **turn L** into Whitewells Lane, signposted 'Blackbrook'. The road drops slightly, then climbs gently up again and after about 1½ miles reaches the hamlet of Belper Lane End (no sign). **Turn very sharp R** just before the Bull's Head, signposted 'Shottle, Alderwasley, Wirksworth'. The road starts climbing again for about ½ mile. At the top of the hill **turn L** into Wilderbrook Lane (no signpost), then after about 200 yds **turn sharp R**, ignoring the tarred surface footpath that goes straight on.

After about a mile – and some welcome downhill – **bear R** at a fork, signposted 'Ashley Hay, Alport'. The road does a little kink by Dannah Farm and then comes to a T-junction where you **turn R** into Chequer Lane, again signposted 'Ashley Hay, Alport'. Ignore side turnings and keep heading for the radio masts on Alport Heights. At the farm buildings at the foot of the hill that the masts are on, **fork R** on Alport Lane. At the top of the hill – after about 300 yds – **turn R** on the access road, which soon becomes a stony path, leading the few yards to the Alport Heights viewpoint.

From the viewpoint, go back to the road and **turn R** for maybe 100 yds to a minor crossroads. **Turn L** into Malins Common Lane, signposted 'Ashley Hay, Idridgehay'. This descent goes on for about 1½ miles and is quite steep in places. Ignore all side turnings; near the bottom the road crosses a disused railway – which there is talk of reopening –

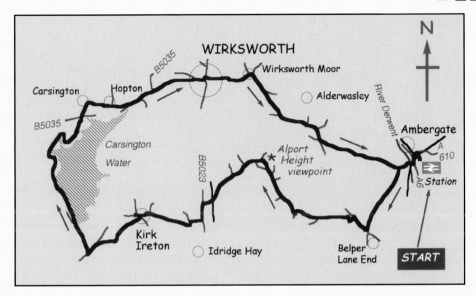

to reach a T-junction with the B5023. **Turn L**, signposted 'Duffield', for about 500 yds, then **turn R**, signposted 'Kirk Ireton, Callow'. The road makes a sharp left-and-right kink, then climbs, very steeply at first, to Kirk Ireton.

At the small green by the church in this attractive little village go straight on, signposted 'Callow, Hopton', and at the far end of the village, and just after the Barley Mow inn, **turn L**, signposted 'Blackwall (only)'. **Keep R** at the road fork at Pebble Cottage, following signs for 'Blackwall'. This is an up-and-down road, through the few cottages which are Blackwall, then – ignoring a minor road to the right – down to a T-junction with a much wider road. **Turn R**, signposted 'Wirksworth, Matlock, Carsington Water' to climb over a slight hill. At the brow

of the hill the masts of boats on Carsington Water are visible ahead. As the road starts to go downhill again there is a brown tourist sign to 'Millfields' on the right; **turn R**. Here there are picnic tables, toilets, a refreshment kiosk – The Spinnaker – and the start of a cycle route round Carsington Water. Just before the payment meter for the car park, **bear L** on the marked cycle route, at this point a tarred path with white cycle route markings, then make what is almost a U-turn to join a path which goes round the reservoir, keeping the water to your right. Follow this path as it widens out to a brick-paved path, then go **L and R** to join a crushed stone path which runs along the crest of the dam, with the road you were on down on your left. Go through the gap beside a five-barred gate and past the sailing club, where the

33

path moves away from the water, signposted 'Visitor Centre, Water Sports Centre'. Go round various barriers to reach the Visitor Centre, which has a café with outside seating. There are toilets here too.

Beyond the Visitor Centre, with the car park on your left, take the path signposted 'Sheepwash, Wildlife Centre'. Follow the blue cycle route arrows: at several points you have to keep left where footpaths bear right. When the path joins a narrow road, go straight ahead (no signpost) along this high-hedged lane, then follow the car park access road out to the B5035. Go almost straight over, signposted 'Hopton, Carsington'.

The road goes first through Carsington, then **sharp R** into Hopton, continuing for about 1½ miles to a T-junction back at the B5035 once more. **Turn L** on the B-road, signposted 'Wirksworth', and after about ½ mile **turn R** (effectively straight on where the B-road bears left), signposted 'Wirksworth (light traffic only)'. The road climbs slightly, and at the brow of the hill you can see Alport Heights off to the right and the monument at Crich straight ahead.

The road swoops down into the quite bustling little town of Wirksworth. At the T-junction in the centre of Wirksworth by the Hope and Anchor, **turn L** and almost immediately **R** just before the Red Lion on the B5035, signposted 'Whatstandwell, Crich'.

After dipping to the disused railway line, the road climbs quite steeply on a miniature continental pass. At the top of the climb, by the Malt Shovel, follow the road round to the **R**, signposted 'Whatstandwell, Crich', then **turn R** (effectively straight on where the B5035 goes sharp left), signposted 'Breamfield, Alderwasley'.

Follow this road, **bearing R**, signposted 'Belper', and ignoring the turn to Alderwasley to pass the Bear Inn. Ignore two minor left turns, still following 'Belper' signs. At a slightly staggered crossroads about a mile after the Bear Inn, **turn L**, signposted 'Ambergate'. This road is mainly downhill for a couple of miles to the bridge over the River Derwent. At the junction with the A6, **turn L** (no signpost), then shortly **R** on the A610, under the railway arch and **R again**, back to Ambergate Station.

CARSINGTON WATER

It is very large – about 2½ miles from tip to tip – and nestles in a curve into the surrounding hills. There is a range of facilities – including an 8-mile cycle path all the way round. The Visitor Centre with its café is at the western end of the Water.

WIRKSWORTH

The compact stone town of Wirksworth was, from Roman times until the end of the 19th century, the centre of the English leadmining industry. The peak of the industry's prosperity was in the 17th and 18th centuries and many of the town's pleasingly-proportioned buildings date from that time.

Hole in the Wall and Osmaston Park

29 miles

By contrast with the uplands of the Peak, this route seems to go through almost continuous parkland, with clear streams and flower-fringed shady lanes. It's essentially a domestic and gentle countryside but really quite a rolling landscape with one or two hidden villages nestling in their valleys. Not as hilly as the Peak routes, but still one to take steadily.

Map: OS Landranger 128 Derby and Burton upon Trent.

Starting point: Duffield Station (GR 346436), which is served by Central Trains stopping services from Derby to Sheffield or Matlock. Duffield is about 5 miles north of Derby. There is limited parking at the station. Alternatively, there is a car park about 400 yds further up the A6, off Golf Lane (GR 343443).

Short cuts: There are numerous opportunities for shortening the route – too many to quote in detail but easily worked out from the OS map.

Refreshments: There are more pubs that serve food on the second half of the route than the first: in fact after leaving Duffield there's nothing until Weston Underwood, and then nothing until the Shoulder of Mutton in Osmaston – apart from the Cock Inn in Mugginton and the Jinglers or Fox and Hounds (one pub: two names) in Bradley, both of them just off the route. After that things look up for a while: Shirley, Hollington, Longford (the Ostrich Inn: outside the village but on the route) and Long Lane all boast pubs – then, we're afraid, nothing again for the 7 or so miles back to Duffield. There is a tearoom on Saturday and Sunday afternoons at Kedleston Hall (open 12 noon to 4 pm) but there is an entry charge to the grounds. The only shop we saw – apart from those in Duffield – was a sparsely stocked but friendly post office in Weston Underwood, but there is a similar one just off the route in Longford.

The route: The terrain is definitely rolling, even hilly in places, and almost entirely through farmland. Overall, the route rises on the outward leg (by almost 500 ft) so it's rather easier on the way back, especially with a westerly tail wind. Apart from a short stretch of the A6 at the start and finish through Duffield itself and a couple of crossings of the A52 there is no main road to be negotiated on this route.

From Duffield Station go up Station Approach (the left of the two exits) to the A6. **Turn L** over the railway bridge to cross two sets of pedestrian-controlled lights, then – just after a prominently blue-

In Osmaston Park

labelled Village Store (actually the Co-op) and just before a large brick building – **turn R** by a memorial with a flagpole into Wirksworth Road; there's no other signpost. At the B5023 at the end of Wirksworth Road, **turn L** and then **immediately R** into Cumberhills Road, signposted 'Quarndon, Kedleston'. This is quite a stiff climb to begin the day's ride but you'll reap the reward later. About a mile past the top of the climb you go down to an oblique T-junction, where you **turn R**, signposted 'Kedleston, Weston, Hulland'. The road goes gently downhill alongside Kedleston Park and then climbs a bit more steadily to Weston Underwood. At the foot of the slope through the village, **turn L**, signposted 'Mugginton'. This narrow little road climbs – between walls of white cow-parsley on the late spring day we rode along it – to Mugginton, where you **turn L** at the T-junction on Church Lane, signposted 'Mercaston', down to the Mercaston Brook and back up again to another T-junction. **Turn R**, still signposted 'Mercaston' to follow the hillside above the Mercaston Brook.

For all its prominence on the signposts, Mercaston is a sparse scattering of a few houses, with no village sign. Just beyond a right-

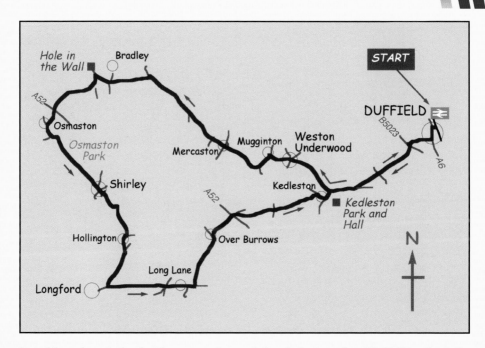

hand bend and the bridge over the brook, **fork L**, signposted 'Brailsford, Bradley', and after about 200 yds, at a crossroads with quite a wide road, go straight on, signposted 'Bradley'. About 600 yds later there's another junction: follow the road markings round to the **R**, signposted 'Bradley' again, and at the next T-junction nearly a mile further on, **turn R**, signposted for 'Bradley' once more. After a slight drop to cross a stream valley there's quite a tough little climb up to a junction – marked as The Knob on the OS map – where you **fork L**, still signposted 'Bradley'.

Just before the village of Bradley, which lies off to the right (no village sign on this road at least), and just past the workshop on the

left of chairmaker N. Tolley, **fork L**. The fork itself isn't signposted but it is obviously the base of a triangle with the signpost (to 'Ednaston') by a bright yellow road grit bin about 100 yds up to the right, at the apex. After about 250 yards, the road markings bear round to the left but the route **bears R** (effectively straight on) into Hadley Lane, signposted 'Moorend'. This little lane is a short but rather stiff climb up to Hole in the Wall; the house with the road through it is just on the right.

At the T-junction by the parish noticeboard, **turn L**, signposted 'Edlaston, Brailsford', and then in about ¼ mile, in Moorend, **fork R**, signposted 'Osmaston', to go over a cattle grid into some open grazing land. After a second cattle grid the road crosses the end of an old airfield to reach the A52. Go straight over, signposted 'Osmaston, Wyaston', to Osmaston church. **Turn L**, signposted 'Edlaston, Wyaston', through the village – from the uniform style of the houses evidently very much an estate village – to a triangular green with a pond.

Fork L to an arrowed sign, 'Bridleway to Shirley', to the left of the lodge gate and the main drive. This is a firm-based gravel track with the possibility of one or two muddy patches after wet weather. After about ½ mile the track drops to cross a tarred drive, signed on a tree 'Shirley straight on'. It continues past the head of a lake, and also past a disused mill. The climb up from the mill through beech and oak woods is steep and sandy: you might have to walk the first bit (we did!). About 400 yds after the top of the steep section the track goes round a gate, drops past some buildings and then goes up for about 100 yds to another gateway where it becomes a tarred road. After about ½ mile this road meets the 'main' village road at a bend; go straight on into Shirley.

Just past the church on the left and the Saracen's Head on the right, **fork L**, signposted 'Hollington, Longford'. There is a very minor crossroads after about 200 yds; go straight on, still signposted 'Hollington, Longford'. At the first T-junction in Hollington, **turn R** on Main Street (no signpost) which bears round to the left for about a mile to another T-junction, opposite the sign for the Ostrich Inn. **Turn L**, signposted 'Long Lane, Kirk Langley', over the bridge to follow this Roman road for about 2½ miles.

It's quite a grinding climb and, just as you begin to feel that this really is the long lane that has no turning, you enter the village of Long Lane, where the Three Horseshoes is very tempting. At the top of the slope up from the village, just past a prominent orange sign for the Cats' Protection League shelter, **turn L**, signposted 'Over Burrows'. The well-groomed hamlet of Over Burrows boasts no village sign but at a small triangular green by the entrance to the park and big house follow the road markings round to the **R**, signposted 'Kirk Langley'.

At the A52 go straight across, signposted 'Kedleston'. From this little road there's a broad view over to the hills on the far side of the Trent valley and Charnwood Forest, followed by a tremendous downhill run to the valley of the stream we last met as the Mercaston Brook, now the Cutler Brook. At the T-junction at the foot of the hill, **turn R**, signposted 'Kedleston', to go past the entrance to Kedleston Hall and over the Cutler Brook up to a T-junction by a prominent white house, The Smithy. **Turn R**, signposted 'Quarndon, Derby'.

You are now back on the outward route for the last few miles. After about ¾ mile, **turn L**, signposted 'Duffield, Windley': the climb that was a bit of a shock to the system on the way out is transformed into a glorious swoop down to Duffield in this direction. At the junction with the B5023, go **L and R** into Wirksworth Road, signposted 'Duffield village'. At the junction with the A6, **turn L** at the 'Stop' sign on Town Street. Go past two sets of pedestrian-controlled lights and over the railway bridge, then immediately after it **turn R** into Station Approach back to Duffield Station.

• •

HOLE IN THE WALL
The intriguingly named Hole in the Wall is more or less just that: the road – which was formerly gated – actually passes through a house at Moorend, Bradley.

OSMASTON
Osmaston Park is a park without its great house: Osmaston Manor was built in 1849 and demolished as recently as 1964 when the family that owned it moved away. Now the bridleway through the park towards Shirley drops through open grassland to a lake, climbing back through woodland to rejoin the road. Osmaston is very much an estate village with its neatly uniform cottages, leading down to a green with a traditional village duckpond.

KEDLESTON HALL
Kedleston Hall is a mansion built in the classical style in the mid-18th century for the Curzon family who have lived in the area since the 12th century. It is set in a 400-acre park with lakes formed by a series of weirs across the brook that our route follows on its outward section (one that changes its name, as several do in this part of the world, according to the village it's passing through). The park is a mixture of open parkland, grazing and fairly open woodland. Kedleston Hall, gardens and park now belong to the National Trust and are open to the public; times and days vary according to the season – telephone 01332 842191 for details. Unlike the National Trust parks on our other routes there is a charge to enter the park.

The Erewash Canal, Nutbrook Trail and Dale Abbey

26 or 20 miles

This route criss-crosses the Nottinghamshire-Derbyshire border as it follows the valley of the River Erewash north from Long Eaton along the recently-established Nutbrook Trail. A walking and cycling trail, it has the distinction of having a smooth tarred surface for much of its length and leads to Shipley Country Park. The route back visits the ruins of 13th-century Dale Abbey.

Map: OS Landranger 129 Nottingham and Loughborough.

Starting point: Long Eaton Station (GR 480322). Trains run to Long Eaton from Nottingham, Beeston (Central Trains), Leicester and Loughborough (Midland Mainline), Derby (Central Trains and Midland Mainline). The station has quite a large pay-and-display car park. Long Eaton is about halfway between Nottingham and Derby.

Alternative starting points/short cuts: You could also start and finish at the Shipley Country Park Visitor Centre (GR 431452); in this case, unless you were absolutely dying to visit Long Eaton, it would be best to turn north on to the Nutbrook Trail at Sandiacre at the point where the return route joins the canal towpath, shortening the total distance by about 6 miles. A similar shortening could be achieved by starting and finishing at the canal bridge in Sandiacre (GR 479364).

Refreshments: There are cafés and tearooms at Shipley Country Park and at Dale Abbey (detailed in the text). Refreshments are also sometimes available at Sandiacre Lock. There are one or two pubs along the canal, and in Mapperley, West Hallam, Stanley, Dale Abbey and Stanton-by-Dale. There are village shops in Mapperley, Stanley and Stanton-by-Dale.

The route: The terrain is flat for most of the way, becoming more rolling after Shipley Country Park with one or two definite climbs around Stanley and Dale Abbey, then flat again once back in the Erewash valley. The canal section features a number of barriers; these are ostensibly to keep motorcycles off the towpath but also make it rather difficult for cyclists with trailers, child seats, tandems or even heavily laden solo bikes. Two or more people travelling together, however, should have no problem in getting these machines round the obstacles. Apart from three straight-over crossings, there is no main road on this route.

The Erewash Canal near Sandiacre

From Long Eaton Station, go over the roundabout to join Tamworth Road, the B6540 (signed as being traffic calmed), and continue along it to go over a canal bridge. Just beyond the bridge the cycle lane leads to a shared-use (foot and cycle) path beside the road; this later rejoins the road as a marked cycle lane where the canal veers away to the left. Continue through the main shopping area as far as a roundabout. Go straight over into Midland Street, signposted 'Sandiacre' with a blue pedestrian and cycle route sign (there are alternative light-controlled crossing facilities if you don't want to tackle the roundabout). Pass between the

Town Hall, to the left, and Asda, on the right.

About halfway along the frontage of Asda, the Nutbrook Trail bears off to the left. Join the Trail here. After a short distance it makes a **L and R dogleg** manoeuvre: stay on the tarred path. Eventually the path surface changes to compacted cinder and at a sign welcoming you to the River Erewash and Toton Washlands go through a metal barrier on the widest path, with the river to the right. This path eventually climbs onto a bank, with the canal to the left, and **bears R** to follow the line of the canal, emerging through a hedge at

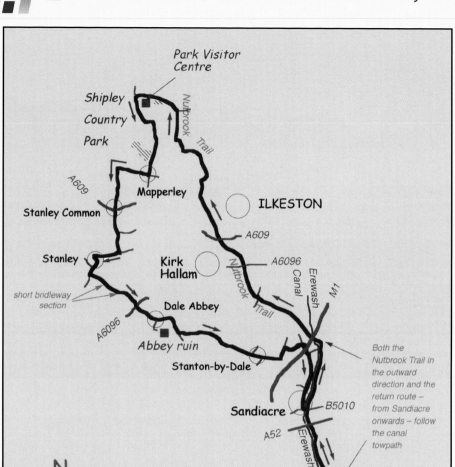

Dockholm Lock (not, apparently, named on the ground) where the Trail joins the towpath proper.

Follow the towpath through Sandiacre for about 2½ miles to pass under the M1 and then under a disused railway. Shortly after this, at the next lock and crossing of the canal, **turn L** to follow the Nutbrook Trail signs to cross and leave the canal. The Trail has a good tarred surface and runs for about a mile through a former industrial area, emerging to cross a minor road. Go through the yellow-and-black-striped barriers and continue on the Trail (signed, but rather inconspicuously from this direction).

The run-down industrial landscape soon gives way to more attractive surroundings, with the former rail bed of the Trail running at first in a cutting. After about 2 miles there is a fork in the path: the left-hand fork leads to a small and quite attractive lake and picnic area known as 'The Beauty Spot'; the right-hand fork is the continuation of the Trail (unsigned here, but the signs resume after a barrier). Shortly after this the route leaves the old railway line and becomes more winding and undulating, passing through some attractive open countryside with water features; there are also plenty of seats for picnics or just a rest. The path passes the houses of Shipley Common on the right and the rides of the American Adventure

theme park come into view ahead.

A number of footpaths leave to left and right, but the Trail remains the only tarred path and is quite obvious. After a few twists and turns, it curves round to the left with a bank on the right, the edge of the American Adventure car park. At the next T-junction **turn R**; there's a wooden 'Nutbrook Trail' fingerpost pointing back the way you've come. Follow this path for about 200 yds; it bears round to the right quite sharply and another path leads to the left.

Turn L, signposted 'Visitor Centre, Shipley Hill' (low wooden sign), and follow this tarred path as it skirts the perimeter fence of the theme park, then goes downhill into a wood, followed by a slight climb to join a minor road. **Turn L** by the Lakeside Business Centre following the 'Nutbrook Trail' sign and continue for about ½ mile until you can see a lake to your left. The path surface changes to a firm gravel track as you pass the lake. Continue straight on to the far end of the lake then, at a post with a red-and-white pattern on it, **bear L** on a path across an open grassy stretch to follow signs up to the Visitor Centre (where there is a cafeteria and the facilities include an information display, toilets, a children's play area, picnic tables and cycle hire).

Leave the Visitor Centre by the path which passes between the children's playground and the cycle hire building and follow this path through the park, keeping straight on to a gated T-junction with a road which has been downgraded to a bridleway. Go through the gate and **turn L**, signposted 'Shipley Hill', for about 300 yds (mind the potholes!) to another gated T-junction with a rather better-surfaced road. **Turn R**; on the left after you have turned there is a tearoom and tea garden in the old Lodge (generally less crowded than the Visitor Centre cafeteria but more restricted opening times).

Continue up a slight hill, through a small wood, then into an open grassy area with wide views. The road goes downhill to pass Mapperley Reservoir and up the hill into Mapperley village. At the crossroads in the centre of the village, by the shop and post office, **turn R** into Main Street past the Black Horse. Follow this road for about 1½ miles (it bears sharply left at one point) to a crossroads with the main A609 at Stanley Common.

Go straight over into Station Road and after about 500 yds follow the road round to the **R** past the White Hart; after another 500 yds **turn R** (signposted 'Stanley, Breadsall') into Stanley, following the road round to the **L** past the church, then **bearing** L again (signposted 'Breadsall, Chaddesden') down to the former Bridge Inn, which is now Bridge Cottage with a pub-

style sign. **Turn L** on Dale Road (unsignposted) and where the tarred road stops continue straight on through the gate on the bridleway. At the third gate, **bear L** onto the tarred road and **turn R** for about 600 yds to a crossroads with the A6096. Go straight over into Arbour Hill, signposted 'Dale Abbey, Stanton-by-Dale', and down the hill into Dale Abbey village. (For teashops and the ruins of Dale Abbey **turn R** opposite the Carpenter's Arms into a road named The Village and marked as a no through road. The teashop options, both on the right, are the Gateway Christian Centre – open 2.30 pm to 5 pm on Sundays and spring and summer bank holidays (information: Rev Ian Gooding, 0115 932 4584) – and the Dale Abbey Tea Rooms at The Friar's House, open Wednesday to Friday and Sunday, mornings and afternoons.)

The route itself continues straight on at the Carpenter's Arms along Moor Lane and bears right uphill to a junction. **Turn L** into Dale Road, signposted 'Stanton-by-Dale', and follow this road for about 1½ miles to the Chequers Inn, Stanton-by-Dale. **Turn R** into Main Street, signposted 'Risley, Sandiacre'. After about 250 yds, **turn L** on Quarry Hill (effectively straight on where the road you're on bears right) signposted 'Stanton', and go down the hill for just over ½ mile. Where the road flattens out, **turn R**, signposted

'Sandiacre, Long Eaton', on a minor road which crosses the golf course. At the next T-junction, **turn R**, signed 'Long Eaton, Sandiacre', to pass under the M1 and continue straight on into Sandiacre to a staggered crossroads with the B5010 at traffic lights.

Turn L over the canal bridge and at the foot of the slope down from the bridge **turn R** to join the Erewash Canal towpath, following the blue pedestrian and cycle sign for 'Long Eaton'. Continue along the towpath towards Long Eaton, following Nutbrook Trail signs. At the second lock, after about ½ mile (Dockholm Lock but not, apparently, named on the ground), the Nutbrook Trail leaves the towpath. Continue on the towpath for about a further 1¼ miles until the canal runs alongside a road on its left, opposite a large comprehensive school. At the point where the canal passes under this road, leave the towpath and join the road, the B6540, Tamworth Road, **turning R** along the on-road cycle lanes to pass over the canal bridge. These lanes extend only over the bridge, but you continue on this road to a small roundabout;

Long Eaton Station is ahead, to the right.

● ● ● ● ● ● ● ● ● ● ● ● ● ● ● ● ● ● ●

MAPPERLEY
This small village – not to be confused with the former village of the same name which is now a suburb of Nottingham – is one of a very few in Derbyshire still to have a set of village stocks. These were boards, into which the victim's legs could be locked, and were used to punish minor crimes such as drunkenness or failure to observe the Sabbath, by leaving the perpetrator subject to humiliation, abuse – and any rubbish that might be thrown.

THE EREWASH CANAL
The Erewash Canal was built between 1777 and 1779 to transport coal from the coalfields of the Erewash valley down to the River Trent. It is just under 12 miles long and runs south from Langley Mill (about 3 miles north-east of Shipley Country Park) to Trent Lock, just south of Long Eaton. The 3½-mile out-and-home trip to Trent Lock from Long Eaton Station makes an interesting diversion. Go south-west from the station on the B6540, Tamworth Road, and after about 300 yds turn left into Netherfield Road. At the end of Netherfield Road turn left over the level crossing on the dead-end Lock Lane to the lock (where there is a canalside pub).

9

North of the Dove

20 miles

T his route, mostly through gently rolling farmland, is one of those where the main pleasure is in the riding – cycling through the quiet countryside and sleepy villages of south-west Derbyshire – rather than calling on noted places of interest. That doesn't mean to say that the route has no points of interest, but the diversions are likely to be in the detail: the unexpected glimpses of a view to distant hills, or down to a brook running through green meadows, or the worn texture of a village wall or old stone bridge. The River Dove which bounds the route to the south and west is a far more mature and placid river than the turbulent youth that rushes through the Peak District's celebrated Dove Dale, and its countryside shares this calm.

Map: OS Landranger 128 Derby and Burton upon Trent.

Starting point: Tutbury and Hatton Station (GR 216297), which is served by Central Trains services from Nottingham and Derby to Uttoxeter, Stoke on Trent, Crewe and Manchester Airport. There is a free car park about 200 yds north of the station, by the mini-roundabout. Hatton is about 7 miles south-west of Derby.

Short cuts: There are numerous opportunities for shortening the route – too many to quote in detail but easily worked out from the OS map.

Refreshments: Be warned – refreshment spots are sparse on this route. There are several pubs that serve food in Hatton and rather more in Tutbury, across the river. There is a pub at Longford, the Ostrich, but it's about ½ mile off the route towards Derby, and pubs actually *on* the route at Marston Montgomery, between Harehill and Boylestone (the Rose and Crown), and Church Broughton (the Hollybush which serves drinks only and is not open at lunchtime on Monday to Thursday). The 'PH' marked on the OS map at the A515 crossing just after Great Cubley is no longer a pub. When the site is open, there's a tearoom at Tutbury Castle and a café (closed on Sunday) in Hatton where the route crosses the A511 a mile after the start. There are shops in Hatton and Tutbury and a small shop is signed just off the route to the left in Great Cubley.

The route: The terrain is gently rolling, almost entirely through farmland. Apart from a short stretch at the start through Hatton itself and a couple of crossings of the relatively minor A515 there is no main road to be negotiated on this route.

Longford Mill

From the north side Tutbury and Hatton station exit – the side where there is a small Metro supermarket – **turn north** on the A511 through Hatton. Shortly after, go straight on at a mini-roundabout, signposted 'Uttoxeter, Derby', continuing for about a mile to a crossroads with traffic lights by the Falcon Inn. Go straight on into Malthouse Lane and at a T-junction after about ¼ mile, **turn R** (no signpost). At the next T-junction **turn L** into Sutton Lane, signposted 'Church Broughton, Longford', to go over the A50 trunk road by a bridge, then continue for about 1½ miles to a crossroads.

Turn R, signposted 'Sutton on the Hill', to cross the Sutton Brook by an attractive stone bridge and ride up into Sutton village, where you **turn L** again, signposted 'Trusley, Thurvaston, Longford'. After about ¼ mile, at the top of a slight slope, take the **first L**, signposted 'Thurvaston, Longford', continuing for about 600 yds to a minor crossroads. **Turn L** into Longford Lane, signposted 'Lower Thurvaston, Longford'. The road climbs gently at first and over the brow the southernmost hills of the Peak District appear on the horizon ahead; there are also several places further along the route – marked on our sketch map – where a similar view opens up.

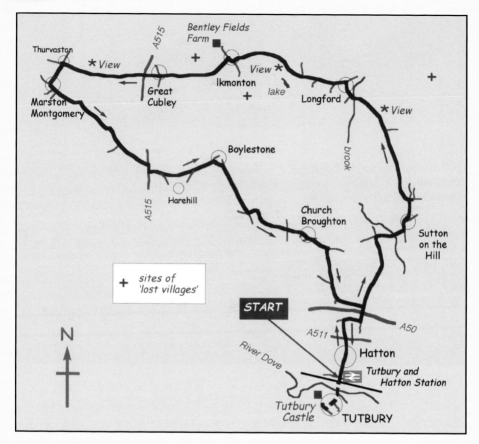

After another mile or so the road bears round to the left to cross the stream, by now renamed the Longford Brook, by a couple of little stone bridges into Longford. Just over the bridges follow the road as it bears round to the right as Main Street. At the end of the village, **turn L**, signposted 'Alkmonton, Cubley' to pass alongside the grounds of Longford Hall. You then climb steadily for a couple of miles to Alkmonton with views over to the left of an attractive small lake about halfway along.

Just beyond the church in Alkmonton, **turn R**, signposted 'Yeaveley, Cubley', and then take the **first on the L**, signposted 'Cubley'. Continue through Great Cubley and up to the A515; go straight over (**slight L/R dogleg**) signposted 'Thurvaston, Marston Montgomery'. After about 1½ miles – in Thurvaston, though there's no indication of the fact on the ground, and it's not the same Thurvaston as appeared on signposts earlier on – **turn L**, signposted 'Marston Montgomery'.

In Marston Montgomery, **turn L** opposite the Crown Inn, just after the church, signposted 'Waldley, Somersal'. Continue along this road, following signs for Sudbury as far as the A515. **Turn R** on the main road, signposted 'Lichfield, Uttoxeter, Sudbury', and then **almost immediately** L, signposted 'Boylestone, Church Broughton'. Follow this road for about 1½ miles to Boylestone – passing on the way the Rose and Crown, one of the rare pubs on this route, and one that does food. In Boylestone, follow the road round to the **R**, signposted 'Sapperton, Church Broughton', and follow the same signs in **turning R** at the next T-junction. At the first minor crossroads **turn L** into Sapperton Lane, signposted 'Church Broughton', and at the next one about a mile later, go straight over on Church Road into Church Broughton.

Continue past the church, now on Main Street, signposted 'Sutton, Hatton, Longford'. About ¼ mile beyond the village, take the **first R** into Bent Lane, signposted 'Hatton'. This road bears round to the left parallel to the main A50 and then comes to a T-junction. **Turn R** to pass over the A50: you are now retracing your wheelmarks on the outward route. **Take the first R**, Breach Lane, and then the **first L** (no sign) after about ¼ mile. This leads directly to the traffic lights then along Station Road into Hatton and back to the station.

To detour to Tutbury Castle, go over the level crossing and then over the River Dove, the boundary with Staffordshire. At a medium-sized roundabout (Tutbury Mill picnic area on the right) go straight on, signposted 'Tutbury Castle', and then **turn R** at a T-junction, still signposted 'Tutbury Castle'. This road climbs and after about 200 yds, by a little triangular green, **bear R**, and up, still signed for the Castle. For details of the Castle's opening times, phone 01283 812129.

• •

LOST VILLAGES
Throughout the East Midlands the Ordnance Survey maps show a scattering of antique cross symbols and gothic type, marking the sites of vanished villages. There are three close to the route, marked on our sketch map: Osleston, Alkmonton and Hungry Bentley. The commonest factors for a village's demise were disease and pestilence – the Black Death or Great Pestilence of the 1340s killed between a third and a half of England's population in a matter of months – or deliberate clearance by landlords, either to create parks or make way for extensive sheep rearing.

TUTBURY CASTLE
Tutbury Castle, which sits in a commanding position on a bluff overlooking the River Dove, is mainly notable as one of the places the unfortunate Mary, Queen of Scots was imprisoned on her enforced travels around the country before her execution.

10

Melbourne, Repton and Calke Abbey

16 miles

This ride is south of the River Trent, for many people the border between the
south and north of England (though we know it's the East Midlands). Over a
thousand years ago it was even more of a border, marking the northern limit of
the Kingdom of Mercia. The route offers a mix of river valley scenery and farmland,
with an especially attractive section through the park of Calke Abbey towards the end.

Map: OS Landranger 128 Derby and Burton upon Trent.

Starting point: The parish church of St Mary and St Michael, Melbourne
(GR 389250), by the entrance to Melbourne Hall. There is a car park nearby, and
a tearoom and toilets at the Hall craft centre opposite the church. The nearest
main line railway station is Derby, about 7 miles just west of north in a straight
line, from which there is a rather circuitous cycle route to Melbourne.
Alternatively you could travel to Willington Station on the line from Derby to
Burton upon Trent, starting and finishing the route at Repton, about 1½ miles
from Willington by the B5008. (Note, though, that Willington is an unstaffed
station with rather a lot of steps up to the platform and no ramps.)

Short cuts: It would be difficult to shorten the route significantly without cutting
out one or more of the points of interest.

Refreshments: There are pubs in Melbourne, Ingleby, Milton, Repton and
Ticknall. There are teashops in Melbourne (at Melbourne Hall craft centre, and the
Welcome Café in the centre) at Brook Farm just as you enter Repton, and at Calke
Abbey. There is a small café at Foremark Reservoir and the village store in Ticknall
does hot drinks and rolls. There are shops in Melbourne, Repton and Ticknall.

The route: The terrain is quite rolling, though the hills aren't very long. Apart
from two short stretches of the relatively minor A514 in Stanton by Bridge and
Ticknall there is no main road to be negotiated on this route.

From Melbourne parish church of
St Mary and St Michael and the
entrance to Melbourne Hall **turn L**
past the Blue Bell inn and at the
top of the hill **turn R**, signposted
'Stanton by Bridge, Derby'. This
road rolls downhill through
Melbourne and then climbs gently
to the junction with the B587.
Turn R, signposted 'Derby', and
continue on the B587 where it goes
sharp **L and R** by the White House
pub, on Derby Road.

The gateway to Repton School

After about ½ mile the road joins the A514 at Stanton by Bridge (traffic on the A-road has to give way) and about another 300 yds later **turn L** (no signpost) opposite a cottage called High Standing. This road climbs westwards out of the village and over the brow of a hill down to a T-junction, with the River Trent straight ahead. **Turn L** with the river on the right (no sign) and shortly afterwards the road begins to climb gently to the hamlet of Ingleby. In the village the road bears round to the left and climbs more steeply away from the Trent for about 300 yds. At the first minor crossroads **turn R**, signposted 'Foremark, Repton,

Milton'. This gently rolling road along the flank of the hill gives extensive views over the Trent. After about 2 miles it bears round to the left and climbs to Milton.

At the junction by the Coach House pub **bear R**, signposted 'Repton'. The road drops steadily into the large village of Repton and bears sharply round to the left into Brook End. Continue uphill on Brook End and after about 200 yds **fork L** up Boot Hill by the Boot Inn. At the T-junction at the top, **turn L** (no signpost) and then after about ¼ mile, soon after the Bull's Head on the right, and just after the vet's on the left, **turn L** into Pinfold Lane. This

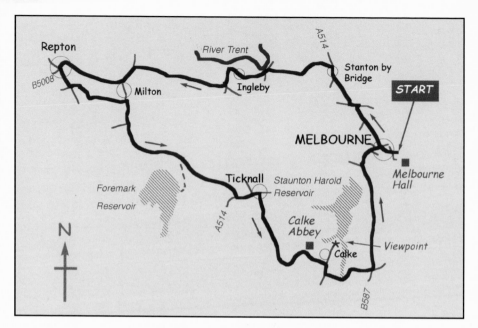

climbs at first and then drops to the south end of Milton. **Turn R** at the T-junction after the small green (no signpost). Ignore the first entrance to Foremark Reservoir after about 1 mile and continue for another ¾ mile to the next.

To make a detour to the reservoir, **turn R** following the brown tourist signs just after Bendalls Farm on the right. At the top of the short but quite stiff hill, the first turn-off to the right leads to a picnic site beside the broad reservoir, while straight ahead leads to more picnic and children's play areas and to the small café kiosk.

Back on the route, continue eastwards, with the spire of Ticknall church visible ahead to the left. At the T-junction with the A514 **turn**

L, signposted 'Derby, Ticknall', and almost immediately enter Ticknall village. Just before the road goes through a stone arch **turn R**, signposted to 'Calke Abbey'. The road follows an impressive avenue of limes to a cattle grid by a gatehouse. The park now opens out and the road swoops down, climbs and then bears sharply round to the left towards Calke Abbey.

Unless you're visiting the house, gardens, shop or restaurant, **turn sharp R**, signposted 'One-way traffic exit'. Follow the one-way signs past the church, then **fork R** to the park exit. At the exit, the route goes **R** through Calke village; to the left there is a short dead-end road to a viewpoint over Staunton Harold Reservoir. Just after the village **turn L**, signposted

'Melbourne, Lount, All major routes', to swoop down across a narrow arm of the reservoir, followed by quite a stiff wooded climb up to the B587.

Turn L on the B587, signed 'Melbourne, Derby', down at first then up and into Melbourne. The road becomes High Street; follow this past a church and an ornate covered seat, then **bear R** into Church Street, signposted 'Melbourne Hall, Wilson', down to return to the parish church and the starting point of the route.

MELBOURNE

The route starts close to the entrance to Melbourne Hall and Gardens, which are open to the public – the gardens on Wednesdays and weekends from April to September, and the Hall during August only. However, it is possible to enjoy the fine setting of the Hall at any time by following the footpath round the north-east side of its lake. The early 17th-century Hall is notable for being the home of the 19th-century Prime Minister William Lamb who became Viscount Melbourne, and after whom the city of Melbourne in Victoria, Australia is named. Note that the name of the Derbyshire original is still pronounced in full, although the Australian version has become 'Melb'n'. The impressive 12th-century church which is also close to the start of the route is one of the finest examples of a Norman parish church in the country. Melbourne was the home of Thomas Cook whose name was to become synonymous with packaged tours. He would be unlikely to recognise today's sex, sun and alcohol trips, though: his first excursion was a special

train laid on in 1841 to carry participants to a temperance meeting in Loughborough.

REPTON

The large village of Repton has something of a cloistered air about it. It was a monastic settlement from the 7th century until the Dissolution of the Monasteries in 1538, after which much of the 12th-century priory was destroyed. Part of it – the guest house – survived and is now part of Repton public school which dominates the village. The village cross, the centrepiece of the village, is said to be the spot where Christianity was first preached in the East Midlands in AD 653. Later the space around it became the site of a market and fair up to the late 1800s. One of the more notorious transactions was in 1848 when a man brought his wife, with a halter round her neck ready to be harnessed, and offered her for sale for a shilling – probably equivalent to something like £20 today.

CALKE ABBEY

Calke Abbey – which is a National Trust property – is unusual in that virtually no alterations have been made to the early 18th-century baroque house. When the National Trust took it over they described it as 'a time capsule', which has been preserved: much of the interior is as it was in the 1880s. Calke was the home of a private and eccentric family of avid collectors: collections of birds, ornaments, paintings and family mementos are all displayed in a rare example of a country house in decline. The Abbey is open to the public from the end of March to the end of October, except on Thursdays and Fridays. For cyclists, though, the main attraction is the vast 600-acre park in which it stands, offering nearly 2½ miles of rolling almost traffic-free road from Ticknall to Calke – and incorporated into our route.

53

11

South-west Derbyshire

22 miles

The southernmost tip of Derbyshire has much more in common with neighbouring Leicestershire than with the north of the county. This route begins with a meander along the Trent valley – a much smaller river here than where we meet it on some of the later routes – and then wanders through several workmanlike villages within the area which is now part of the new National Forest.

Map: OS Landranger 128 Derby and Burton upon Trent.

Starting point: Burton upon Trent Station (GR 242232). Trains from Derby, Nottingham and Birmingham call at Burton upon Trent Station where there is also a small pay-and-display car park.

Short cuts: It would be difficult to shorten the route significantly without cutting out the pleasant southern villages in the Mease valley.

Refreshments: There are pubs in Burton (of course!), Walton-on-Trent, Edingale, Lullington, Coton in the Elms and Rosliston. There is a teashop at the Rosliston Forestry Centre. There are shops in Burton and its suburbs, also in Walton-on-Trent and Rosliston.

The route: The terrain is gently rolling, one of our easier routes. Apart from the short urban stretches in Burton just after the start there is no main road to be negotiated on this route.

With Burton upon Trent station buildings behind you, **turn R** to leave the station car park, signposted 'Town Centre, Tourist Information' (both pedestrian signs), and go down Station Street past one of the large breweries with which the name Burton is synonymous. At a crossroads with traffic lights, just past Sainsbury's, **turn R** into Guild Street (not very prominently signed). Go straight on through two sets of traffic lights in quick succession, then, at the next set, a minor crossroads just after the Burton Union pub, **turn L** into New Street, signposted 'Tourist Information, Central Area Rooftop'. This leads to a mini-roundabout junction; go straight on into Manor Croft, marked as a no through road. Immediately **bear R** towards Burton College, then **turn R** just before the college sign,

At Rosliston Forestry Centre

keeping the college buildings close on the left.

At the end of the buildings go between some low bollards and immediately **turn L** to join the shared-use cycle route. This is an elevated purpose-built route across the River Trent floodplain which crosses the Trent by the ornate black-and-white Ferry Bridge, prominently dated 1889. After the bridge, the path joins a minor road, The Dingle, which rises gently to a T-junction with Ferry Street. Unfortunately you can't turn left – the way you want to go – but have to **turn R** on one-way Ferry Street, which soon curves round to the left

and becomes two-way, then take the **first turning L**, Frederick Street, up to a T-junction. **Turn L** by an antique shop on the left and an off-licence on the right (no obvious street name here although it is actually Hill Street) for about 100 yds to a further T-junction, with Main Street. **Turn R** (no signpost); the street almost immediately becomes Rosliston Road.

After just over a mile the road crosses a railway; shortly after this, **turn R**, signposted 'Drakelow Power Station, Walton'. Follow this road for about 3 miles to Walton-on-Trent, where, at a T-junction,

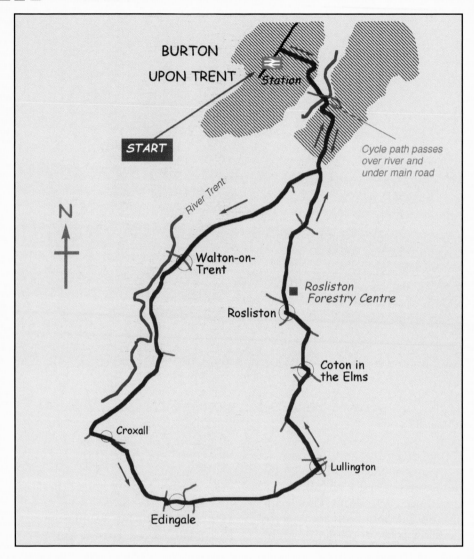

BURTON
UPON TRENT

Station

START

Cycle path passes
over river and
under main road

River Trent

N

Walton-on-
Trent

Rosliston
Forestry Centre

Rosliston

Coton in
the Elms

Croxall

Lullington

Edingale

turn **R** into Main Street, just before
the Shoulder of Mutton. Go
straight on at the next staggered
crossroads, signposted 'Catton,
Croxall', past the White Swan.
Continue on this road, following
signs for Catton and Croxall **round
to the R** by an octagonal house,
after about 1½ miles.

Pass Catton Hall on the right and
about 1½ miles further on, **turn L**
into Croxall Road, signposted
Edingale. After about ¼ mile the
road passes through the well-kept
estate village of Croxall and some 2
miles later reaches Edingale. Go
straight on through Edingale, over
a mini-roundabout at the far end of

the village, and straight on again at the next junction about 1½ miles later, following signs for 'Lullington'. Around here the route enters the area of National Forest.

There's a small hill up to Lullington with its rather imposing church, where you **turn L** opposite the village school, signposted 'Coton'. **Keep L**, following signposts for 'Coton in the Elms', and continue on this road for about a mile to a T-junction; **turn R**, still signposted for 'Coton in the Elms', to reach the village about ½ mile later. Just after the first houses of Coton in the Elms, **turn R**, signposted 'Rosliston, Linton, Overseal', into Mill Street, which runs with its stream first on the left, then on the right to make a pleasing village centre feature. There's also a pub, the Black Horse.

Follow the road where it bears round to the left to leave the village on Burton Road. After ½ mile, just beyond the village sign for Rosliston, **turn L** into Main Street at a mini-roundabout, signposted 'Walton, Burton'. At the far end of the village **bear round to the R**, signposted 'Walton, Burton' again, passing the Bull's Head on the left, then follow signs for 'Burton, Rosliston Forestry Centre'. The Centre is about ½ mile out of the village, with a café and picnic area and nature trails.

Continuing from the Centre back towards Burton, the road begins to go downhill slightly for about 2 miles to the railway bridge where you turned right on the way out. **Bear R** on Rosliston Road to enter Staffordshire and Burton upon Trent. Retrace the outgoing route along Rosliston Road but continue downhill past Hill Street where you came out and then **turn L** into Ferry Street, just before the New Inn. After about 100 yds, **turn R** into The Dingle to go over the Trent and along the cycle path on the causeway.

At the end of the path, **turn R** through the bollards, past the buildings of Burton College and straight on at the mini-roundabout into New Street. At the traffic lights go straight on across Union Street (no longer retracing the outgoing route) to the next traffic lights, where you go straight on again into Moor Street. About 50 yds further on, just before Mulligan's pub on the left, **turn R** into Cross Street to its junction with Station Street. **Turn L** on Station Street back to Burton upon Trent Station.

● ●

THE BASS MUSEUM

Not in Derbyshire, but close to the start of our route, the Bass Museum in Horninglow Street, Burton upon Trent covers the history of the Bass company, brewing and beer. It was opened in 1977 to celebrate the bicentenary of Bass in Burton, their famous red triangle the very first registered trademark. Exhibits include a reconstructed Edwardian bar, the company's historical fleet of horse-drawn and motor vehicles and a working micro-

brewery, producing the traditional ales served in the bars in the museum. It is even licensed for wedding ceremonies! Details: 01283 511000.

THE NATIONAL FOREST

The National Forest is an ambitious project, begun in the 1990s, to create 200 square miles of new forest for the nation across a great swathe of Leicestershire, Derbyshire and Staffordshire, from the outskirts of Leicester to well beyond Burton upon Trent. Some of the project involves restoring the land to what it used to be, since it stretches between the ancient Needwood and Charnwood Forests, but much of it is old coalfields and other former industrial land. Already well over 2,000 acres of derelict mineral workings have been returned to forest and open recreational land. The goal is not to create continuous dense woodland but a mixed countryside of farmland, recreational open land, villages and forest. When the project began, about 6% of the area was covered in woodland; now, with the planting of 4 million trees this has been doubled. And the aim is to plant another 26 million! Our route passes the Rosliston Forestry Centre with its waymarked walks, wildlife hides and National Forest exhibition. The whole of this route, and the previous one from Melbourne (Route 10), lies within the boundaries of the National Forest.

Retford, North Leverton and Clayworth

22 miles

Towards the far north of Nottinghamshire the gentle hills begin to peter out into a flat plain that carries right on up into the Vale of York. It's very much an arable landscape, golden with cornfields in late summer – some of it no doubt waiting to be ground at the still-working Leverton Mill. The Chesterfield Canal wanders though the last part of the journey and there is a chance to visit one (or more!) of its waterside pubs.

Map: OS Landranger 120 Mansfield and Worksop.

Starting point: Retford Station (GR 702803). Sadly, Retford Station – or Stations, since there's an upper one (on the East Coast Main Line) joined to a lower (on the Sheffield–Gainsborough line from Worksop) – is remarkably un-cycle-friendly with sets of steps and quite a long trek to be negotiated in getting from the lower station to the upper, which has the only exit to the outside world. Allow a good five minutes to get from the entrance to the lower station (signed as platforms 3 and 4) if you're coming back to catch a train to Worksop or Gainsborough or beyond. There are also steps to and from the northbound main line platform.

There is some paying car parking by the station and other car parks towards the centre of the town.

Short cuts: It would be difficult to shorten the route significantly without cutting out one or more of the points of interest.

Refreshments: There are pubs in Retford, North Leverton, Sturton le Steeple, North Wheatley, Clayworth (just off the route) and Hayton. There are teashops in Retford and at the Grove Garden Centre (all right then, a coffee shop). There are shops in Retford, North Leverton, between South and North Wheatley, and by the canal just before you get to Clayworth.

The route: Once you've got past Grove the terrain is relatively flat, with one more climb after North Wheatley. (And maybe it was the hot summer afternoon when we rode up through Grove that made the climb up from the River Idle seem harder than we'd expected!) Apart from about 200 yds of the old Great North Road, the A638, soon after the start and about ¼ mile downhill on the A620 at the end there is no main road to be negotiated on this route.

North Leverton Windmill

house number 78, **turn L** (no signpost) into All Hallows Street. Follow the road as it bears round to the right past the church, then, at a point where the river comes close to the road on the left, **turn L** into Goosemoor Lane, over a marked 'weak bridge' (but with no other signpost).

At the junction with the A638, opposite the White Houses pub, **turn R**, signposted 'Newark', and after about 200 yds, **turn L**, signposted 'Grove, Headon, Rampton'. After about 1½ miles – and what felt quite a climb on the hot August afternoon when we first rode this route – **turn L**, signposted 'Grove' (and Grove Garden Centre Coffee Shop). Main Street, Grove continues the climbing theme, and about ½ mile beyond the village broad views to east and south open up. At one point Lincoln Cathedral shows up at the end of its ridge, tastefully framed by two of the (many) power stations in this part of the Trent valley.

From the Retford Station exit, **turn L** and follow the road parallel to the car park and railway – Station Road, though unmarked at this point – for about 200 yds, then **fork L** by a somewhat odd-looking set of white buildings into Westfield Road, which is rather potholed to begin with. Just before the road bends right, **turn L** to walk over the ramped footbridge across the railway. On the far side, at the foot of the footbridge ramp, **turn L**; this is West Carr Road which becomes Ollerton Road though neither is signed at this point.

After about ¾ mile, just before a bend in the road and opposite

The road now begins to go downhill but about ½ mile down, just before a bend, **turn L**, signposted 'Leverton, Sturton'. This road dips and then climbs again to another T-junction. **Turn R**, signposted 'N[orth] Leverton', down the hill, **bearing L** at the next bend in the road, signposted 'North Leverton and Gainsborough'. At the foot of the next slope, Mill Lane, leading to the working windmill, goes off to

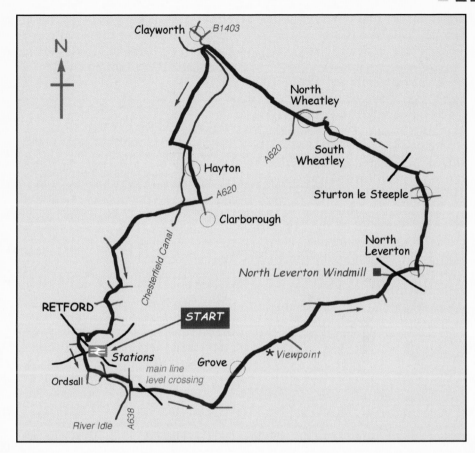

the left; the mill is about 300 yds along this road.

The main route bears round to the right past the 'North Leverton with Habblesthorpe' village sign (claimed to be the longest place-name in England) and under the railway into North Leverton. In the centre of North Leverton, at a crossroads by the Royal Oak, **turn L**, signposted 'Sturton, Gainsborough'. Continue through Sturton le Steeple (whose church doesn't have a steeple but a tower crowned by

about a dozen steeple-ettes) and at the far end of the village follow the road round to the left, then where the major road goes round to the right, go straight on, signposted 'Weatley [sic], Clayworth'.

Continue through the twin villages of South and North Wheatley to a crossroads with the A620 by the Sun Inn. Go straight over, signposted 'Clayworth, Mattersey', climbing at first to the top of Haughgate Hill (it's not as tough as it looks from the crossroads). Then

it's about 1½ miles downhill to the junction with the B1403 on the outskirts of Clayworth, beside the Chesterfield Canal.
Turn very sharp L over the canal, signposted 'Hayton, Retford'. The road follows a flat and rather zig-zag route for about 4 miles into Hayton. At the far end of the village, just before the junction with the A620, **turn R** into Smeath Lane (signposted to the Gate Inn, but no 'official' signpost). Follow this road for about 3 miles (**bearing L** where Tiln Lane comes in from the right) to an oblique T-junction with the A620 on the outskirts of Retford. **Turn R** down the hill (no signpost), and at the foot of the hill **bear L** at the traffic lights on Arlington Way, signposted 'Newark'.

If you want to visit the picturesque Market Place and Cannon Square in the centre of Retford, it's easiest to go straight ahead over the light-controlled pedestrian crossing into the blocked-off Churchgate at this point.

Otherwise, at the fourth set of traffic lights, where London Road, signposted 'Newark', bears round to the L, **turn R** on Albert Road, signposted (rather inconspicuously from this direction) with a station

symbol. After about 500 yds, **turn L** on Victoria Road (the road name sign looks as though it refers to the wrong road), signposted to the station.

● ●

NORTH LEVERTON MILL
There are several windmills in working order in Nottinghamshire but the one at North Leverton is unique: it has been in use ever since it was built by a group of local farmers as the 'Subscription Mill' in 1813. It is still locally owned and is open every afternoon except Thursdays; visitors can buy the wholemeal milled product. The building also houses a small exhibition about mills and milling.

THE CHESTERFIELD CANAL
The Chesterfield Canal, from Chesterfield in Derbyshire to the River Trent at West Stockwith is Nottinghamshire's oldest canal. It was dug in the 1770s, opening in 1777, and numbered 65 locks and two tunnels in its original 46-mile length. It operated fully commercially only until 1863 when the railway company that had bought it decided to allow it to run down, a decline hastened by the collapse of one of the tunnels which effectively cut off the Chesterfield end. It now carries a fair amount of leisure traffic and attracts large numbers of anglers. Most of the canal towpath is not open for cycling although a stretch near Worksop forms part of the 'National Cycle Network' Route 6, some of which features on our Worksop and Clumber Park ride (Route 13).

Worksop and Clumber Park

24, 19 or 16 miles

The highlight of this ride is a visit to Clumber Park, an extensive area of forest and open land now owned by the National Trust and one of the jewels of north Nottinghamshire. The route ventures away from tarred roads in places to see parts of the forest at their best and quietest – all the bridleways are firm-surfaced and easily ridable. The full circuit starts and finishes in the town of Worksop but it's possible to make use of the Robin Hood railway line to finish at Creswell or Whitwell Stations instead, allowing you to avoid the mile of main road after Whitwell – though this means you miss the canal towpath as well.

Map: OS Landranger 120 Mansfield and Worksop.

Starting point: Worksop railway station on the Robin Hood Line from Nottingham (GR 585798) and also served by Northern Spirit trains from Sheffield, Retford and Gainsborough. There is a station car park and other car parks are available in the town centre.

Short cuts: The route distance may be shortened to about 19 miles by returning by train from Whitwell Station or to about 16 miles by returning from Creswell Station, instead of cycling the last bit into Worksop.

Refreshments: There are many cafés and pubs in Worksop and a restaurant and cafeteria in the Clock House at Clumber Park, which gets very crowded at weekends. The Old School Tearoom at Carburton and the Welbeck Abbey Garden Centre are possibilities, plus light refreshments at Creswell Crags Visitor Centre. There are also pubs in most of the villages the route passes through, but as far as we could see no shops on the actual route after Worksop until Whitwell.

The route: The terrain is gentle with the only real bit of climbing through Whitwell village. The route is a mixture of tarred road, firm-surfaced track and path, and good quality canal towpath. There are two stretches of main road: about 500 yds of the A60 after Holbeck (usually quiet) and just over a mile of the A619 after Whitwell. This last can be a bit busy but is downhill in the direction described (and so it doesn't take long).

The street-level exits from Worksop Station are at the level-crossing (eastern) end of the platforms. Once on the road, **turn R** downhill towards the town, straight on at the first set of traffic lights and over the canal bridge. Immediately after the bridge, just past the Lock

By the lake at Creswell Crags

Tavern, **turn L** into Church Walk, **bearing L** on Canal Road, signed as a cycle route (bicycle sign plus a number '6').

After about ¼ mile, this bears round to the **R** to join Priorswell Road, unsignposted at this point but which crosses the canal by a bridge on the left. **Turn R** into Priorswell Road (ignoring the cycle route signs which carry on along the canal towpath), past Worksop Priory on the left, to a T-junction. **Turn L**, signposted 'Manton, Retford', and after about 50 yds take the **first R**, into Lowtown Street which becomes Netherton Road. After about ½ mile, as the road becomes noticeably uphill and within sight of a main-road roundabout, **turn L** by a telephone box on the left into Waverley Way (signed on houses but not visible at this point). After about 100 yds, at a minor crossroads, **turn R** into Cavendish Way which bears round to the left and follow this for about 250 yds. **Turn R** under a green height barrier (signed cycle route, but signs not visible until you have made the turn) and follow the signs **L and R** across a pedestrian bridge over the A57, Worksop bypass. At the far side of the bridge continue on the gravel track to reach a minor road by a golf clubhouse.

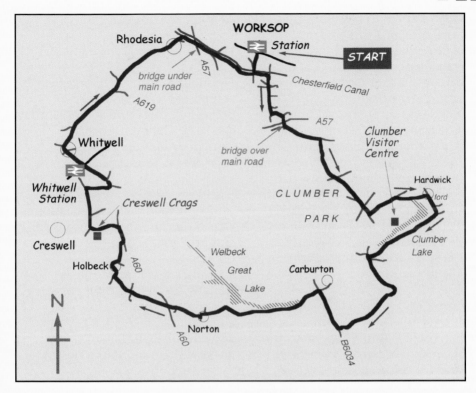

Turn L uphill past Worksop
College and about 300 yds beyond
the College **turn R** past a metal
barrier onto a bridleway signposted
'Public Bridleway to Clumber Park'
with a cycle route sign. This is a
firm-surfaced path through
attractive woodland, which later
becomes a firm-surfaced wider
track. At a tarred road about 500
yds further on, go straight over
past a wooden barrier, still
signposted 'Public Bridleway to
Clumber Park' with a cycle route
sign. After about ¼ mile ignore the
cycle route turn to the right,
continuing on the bridleway for
about 600 yds to a tarred road.
Turn L and shortly after, at a

crossroads with the impressive
lime-tree avenue, continue straight
on, signposted 'Shop, restaurant
and chapel', past a payment kiosk
(no charge for cyclists!). Just after
the kiosk, **turn L**, signposted
'Hardwick village', and at an
unmarked fork a little later follow
the road markings round to the
right. The road passes between two
lakes to reach a T-junction with the
houses of Hardwick Village to the
right. **Turn R** through the village
and then either through a long
ford or over the adjacent
footbridge. Continue up the slope
to a T-junction, and go straight on
past a low wooden pole barrier,
then another, on a firm path for

about 300 yds to reach another tarred road at a third barrier. **Turn R** for about 1¼ miles down to a meeting of roads with the fine arch of Clumber Bridge on the right. **Turn L**, signposted 'South Lodge – no through road' plus a cycle route sign. Just before the barrier approaching the firmly-closed lodge gates, **turn L** to follow the cycle route sign along a path which comes to a T- junction with a bridleway. **Turn R**, signposted 'RUPP to Duncan Wood', still on the cycle route, and follow this firm-surfaced path for just over a mile to the B6034.

Turn R on the B6034 downhill for about ¾ mile and then **turn L**, signposted 'Norton, Cuckney', the Old School Tearoom is on the left. Follow this road past a series of lakes on the right (with a heronry on the far side of the first one) for just over 2 miles to Norton. Just after the road sweeps round to the left at the beginning of the village, **turn R**, signposted 'Worksop', and after about ¾ mile go straight across the A60, signposted 'Holbeck'. Go straight on at an oblique crossroads of very minor roads and up to a T-junction. **Turn R** through Holbeck to reach the A60. **Turn L**, signposted 'Worksop', for about 500 yds and then **turn L** onto a bridleway by a stone lodge (halfway along this stretch the Welbeck Garden Centre and tearoom is signed to the right). At the white barrier the bridleway becomes a footpath to Creswell Crags Visitor

Centre, which is in sight.

From the Visitor Centre follow the exit road to the B6042 and **turn R** for about 400 yds to a fork. **Bear L**, signposted 'Whitwell', past a dolomite quarry and rotary kiln. At the next T-junction **turn R** (unsignposted) under a high bridge to a second T-junction, which has a small triangular green. **Turn L** (again no signpost) gently uphill into Whitwell. (Whitwell Station is signed on the left soon after you enter the village.) In the centre of the village, at a crossroads opposite a weathered war memorial, go straight ahead into High Street, signposted 'Chesterfield'. This climbs quite steeply for perhaps 250 yds to reach a small shady green with an old pump on the right. **Turn R** on the B6043, Worksop Road, signposted – unsurprisingly – 'Worksop'.

The road continues to climb, with quite extensive views to the right over Welbeck and Clumber Parks from the highest point, then drops to the A619. **Turn R**, signposted 'Worksop'. Follow the A619 downhill (care) for about 1 mile and then **turn L**, signposted 'Shireoaks, Thorpe'. Follow this road for some 2 miles to pass **R and L** under a railway bridge into Rhodesia. Continue under the A57, Worksop bypass, and immediately afterwards **turn L** off the road to join the canal towpath, with a cycle route sign.

Turn R under a low bridge (care again!) and ride alongside the canal for about 1¾ miles to the centre of Worksop. Leave the towpath through the KwikSave car park – a seasonal landmark is a moored barge which is a tearoom – and **keep L** parallel to the canal to go through a gap by Walmsley's Suite Superstore (on your left) onto Bridge Place. **Turn L** over two sets of traffic lights to go uphill to the station (you may find it easier to use the pedestrian crossings at the second set of traffic lights, which is a fairly complex junction).

*If you want to return by train from Creswell Station, **turn L** on the B6042 past Creswell Crags themselves (traffic light-controlled one-way working) as far as the A616. **Turn R** on the A616 (signposted 'Clowne') for about 300 yds, then **L** (signposted 'Station' and several other places) to Creswell Station (approaches either side of the railway bridge, depending on which direction you want to travel).

● ●

CLUMBER PARK
Clumber Park was one of the great estates of the area known as the 'Dukeries', because of the number of ducal domains, and is now under the care of the National Trust. Clumber belonged to the Dukes of Newcastle but – unlike the other parks of the Dukeries – the great house is no longer there, demolished over 60 years ago leaving

only its outline now traceable. Parts of the formal garden, the great glasshouse and the walled kitchen garden as well as the vineries remain and are open to the public. The Victorian gothic chapel is a prominent landmark, while the old clock tower now houses a cafeteria, shop and restaurant. The real attraction of Clumber, however, is the 3,800 acres of parkland – a mixture of fine and varied woodland, open space and heathland surrounding an 80-acre lake. The route passes the superb double central avenue of lime trees and there's the chance of cycling through a ford – with a footbridge close by if you don't want to. Cyclists can use the network of 13 miles of tarred roads and many other firm-based tracks and bridleways. Although Clumber attracts many visitors, particularly at summer weekends, moving traffic is light because motorists have to pay to get into the central area and some of the roads are barred to motor traffic; people on bicycles enter free.

CRESWELL CRAGS
The rocky cleft of Creswell Crags straddles the Nottinghamshire and Derbyshire border, with a small lake nestling in between. The caves and rock shelters in the cliffs beside the lake were inhabited at least as long ago as 12,000 years, in late Palaeolithic times, making them some of the oldest habitations in Britain, and the northernmost of that Ice Age period. The caves are not generally open to the public, but guided cave tours are arranged from time to time from the Visitor Centre, where there is an excellent display revealing the history of the Crags, complete with replica cave. In fine weather the lake shore makes a very pleasant grassy picnic spot.

Retford, Tuxford and Laxton

31, 18, 13, or 12 miles

This is our longest route (if you choose to do the whole circuit) and reaches right back in history. It takes us from the old coaching towns of Retford and Tuxford (which is now really only a village) to the only place in England still practising medieval strip culture, where communal land is rotated between the different village farmers year by year. Although it doesn't climb very high the route is quite unexpectedly up-and-down for the first half as it mostly climbs to the villages, then drops to the stream valleys in between.

Map: OS Landranger 120 Mansfield and Worksop.

Starting point: Retford Station (GR 702803) – see Route 12. There is some paying car parking by the station and other car parks towards the centre of the town.

Alternative starting point/short cuts: The route distance may be slashed to about 13 miles by going straight on at Upton on the way out to East Drayton and then following the return directions back to Retford, but this misses out some of the more interesting bits. An alternative would be to start from Tuxford and follow the route as far as East Drayton, turning left at the church there to Upton, then following the 'official' route back to Tuxford. The total distance would be about 18 miles, which could be further cut to 12 by turning left directly back to Tuxford just after Skegby.

Refreshments: There are several cafés and restaurants in the centre of Retford and, as befits a town on the old Great North Road, a number of coaching inns. There are pubs in Askham, East Markham, Tuxford, Egmanton, Laxton, Darlton and East Drayton. There is a café at the garden centre in Grove, about a mile off the route and signed, towards the end of the route. The only village shops we saw were in Tuxford.

The route: The terrain is, as already noted, undulating in places, becoming flatter in the second half which runs closer to the Trent. There are no real main road problems except possibly about 200 yds of the A57 at Darlton.

From the Retford Station exit, **turn L** and follow the road parallel to the car park and railway – Station Road, though not signed at this point – for about 200 yds to fork left by an odd-looking range of white buildings into Westfield Road, which is rather potholed to begin with. Just before the road bends right, **turn L** to walk over the

The open road near Laxton

ramped footbridge across the railway. On the far side, at the foot of the footbridge ramp, **turn L**; this is West Carr Road which becomes Ollerton Road though neither is signed at this point. At the next T-junction, **turn L**, still on Ollerton Road, and continue for about 1 mile.

Take the **first turning L** (not signposted but the road has a weight limit sign) to cross the River Idle into the pretty village of Eaton. At the junction with the Great North Road at the end of the village, **turn L and almost immediately R**, signposted 'Upton, East Drayton'. This road passes Eaton Wood nature reserve and after another 2 miles, in Upton, **turn R** into Askham Lane, signposted 'Askham'.

Continue through Askham, passing under the railway and crossing the A57 to East Markham. In the village go straight on by the Crown Inn into Farm Lane and continue straight on, signposted 'Tuxford', over the A1 to a T-junction with the B1164 (not signposted). **Turn L** and climb through Tuxford; at the top **turn R** by the Newcastle Hotel and **almost immediately R** again into Newcastle Street. Continue on this road, signposted 'Egmanton, Laxton' to the attractive village of Egmanton, then **bear L** following signs for 'Laxton'.

In Laxton, **bear L**, signposted 'Kneesall, Moorhouse', at a grassy triangular green with a spreading chestnut tree. On the left is the Dovecote Inn, in the yard of which is

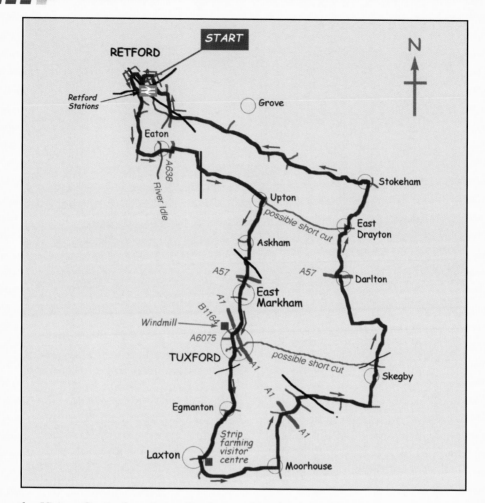

the Visitor Centre housing a display which tells of Laxton's strip farming.

At the foot of the village, **bear L**, signposted 'Moorhouse, Carlton-on-Trent'. After about 2 miles, in the hamlet of Moorhouse, **turn L**, signposted 'Egmanton, Weston', and continue for about 1½ miles to another T-junction. **Turn R**, signposted 'Weston, Newark', to cross over the A1 to the junction with the B1164. **Turn L**, signposted 'Tuxford, Retford', and about 200 yds later **turn R** (signpost broken at the time of survey) over a level crossing beside a disused windmill. About 1½ miles beyond this, **turn L**, signposted 'Skegby, Darlton'. Shortly after the few houses which make up the hamlet of Skegby **turn L and immediately R** (effectively straight on). Follow this road – which has quite a few right-angle bends – to the A57 in Darlton.

Go **L** (no signpost) and after about 200 yds **R**, signposted 'East Drayton'. On the outskirts of East Drayton, **go R** and then bear round to the left on Top Street to a minor crossroads by the church. Go straight on, signposted 'Stokeham', and in Stokeham, **turn L** on Main Street, signposted 'Retford'.

Continue to follow signs to Retford (which means **turning L** at one point, effectively straight on) as far as the junction with the A638, the Great North Road on the outskirts of Retford. **Turn R**, signposted 'Retford', go over the railway bridge and then take the **second L**, Whinney Moor Lane, signposted 'Thrumpton Road Industrial Area'. At the T-junction opposite the Clinton Arms, about ¼ mile past the level crossing, **turn L** (unsignposted) over the River Idle, then **immediately L** into Victoria Road to the station.

• •

RETFORD

The modern town of Retford really comprises two: the old and larger town of East Retford, on the east bank of the River Idle, and West Retford on the other side. Today the village of Ordsall has also been absorbed into the whole. The town's prosperity was enhanced in the 18th century when it was successful in having the Great North Road diverted a couple of miles to the east so that it ran through both Retfords, which became an important coaching community. The fine Market Place and Square is essentially Georgian with a controversial Victorian Town Hall on the fourth side. A feature – prominent enough for the square to be

know locally as 'Cannon Square' – is the heavy Russian cannon captured at the battle of Sebastopol during the Crimean War. The Great North Road has given way to the concrete wilderness of the near-motorway A1, once more diverted to the west of Retford.

TUXFORD

Tuxford is another town, or large village, to owe its former prosperity to its strategic position on the Great North Road. Evidence is still to be found in the large coaching inns at the top of the main street in Market Place, though not many of the shops that must also have been there remain. Less fortunate travellers were those who spent the night in the 1823 brick lock-up in Newcastle Street, on our route, as a result of drunkenness or other misdemeanours. Also near our route, to the north of Tuxford, a prominent landmark is Longbottoms Mill, a restored tower mill which is open to the public from time to time.

LAXTON

Laxton is unique: it is the last village in England where medieval strip culture is practised. At a special Court Leet meeting every November broad strips of the three great fields, which have never been enclosed, are allocated in rotation to farmers for the following year. The basis of the practice was to allow every farmer to have spells on both the best and the worst lands, so that none was unduly favoured or penalised. Since the farmers have never actually owned specific areas of land, the farmhouses are in the village instead of being dispersed and surrounded by their own grounds. A Visitor Centre, beside the Dovecote Inn in the centre of the village, details Laxton's history. There is also a Laxton Trail leading round the fields and the remains of its Norman castle, and a museum of agricultural implements.

15

Southwell's Countryside

22 ,14½ or 13 miles

This route leads out into the gentle countryside of east Nottinghamshire, where the little streams and their valleys are generally known as 'dumbles'. The small town of Southwell where the route starts is dominated by the imposing Minster but the town has many other interesting corners and is also memorable as the home of the Bramley cooking apple. The countryside is a mixture of arable and grazing land with some woodland and parks – while surprisingly the route also visits an oilfield. Less surprisingly it also goes by Nottinghamshire's tiniest pub.

Map: OS Landranger 120 Mansfield and Worksop.

Starting point: Opposite Southwell Minster (GR 702538), in Church Street. Southwell is about 11 miles north-east of Nottingham. There is a car park with toilets opposite the Minster.

Short cuts: The route distance may be shortened to 13 miles by following the outward route to Edingley and then returning to Southwell by the Southwell Trail. Alternatively, you could travel out to Edingley by the Trail and complete the circuit from there, which would make a route of about 14½ miles.

Refreshments: There are several cafés and restaurants in Southwell, and a tearoom at Hockerton. There are also pubs in Halam, Oxton, Edingley, Kirklington, Eakring, Maplebeck, Hockerton and Southwell. There is a village store at the post office in Oxton.

The route: The terrain is rolling with one or two steady climbs; fortunately, you go down the steepest hill – Oxton Bank on the B6386 – not long after the start. The steepest uphill is a pitch of perhaps a couple of hundred yards up to the B6386 after Halam. There are three short stretches of A-road, none of them very busy.

From the car park opposite Southwell Minster, **turn R** to a mini-roundabout by the Saracen's Head, **turn R** (unsignposted), then **almost immediately** L into Queen Street. **Keep L** at the next fork and continue for about 1½ miles into Halam. In Halam **turn L** into Radley Road past the church to climb steadily up the little valley to a T-junction with the B6386. **Turn R**, signposted 'Oxton, Nottingham'.

The road climbs gently at first,

Southwell Minster

then plunges down a twisting hill. The clumps of trees on the left are said to have been planted in the positions of the troops in a Civil War battle here. About 600 yds beyond the foot of the hill, take the **first R** turn, Blind Lane, signposted 'Oxton village'. Follow this road into the village to a T-junction by the Green Dragon in Oxton. **Turn R** into Forest Road, signposted '(A6097) Ollerton'. Go gently uphill for about ½ mile to an oblique crossroads with the A6097.

Turn R on the dual-carriageway A6097, signposted 'Doncaster'. After a further ½ mile, soon after the dual carriageway becomes a

single carriageway and after passing Moorfields Farm on the left, take the first minor road turning on the right, Greaves Lane (otherwise unsignposted). The attractive little lane climbs gently for a short way and then swoops down a pretty valley between high hedges – but watch the bends!

After about 1½ miles follow the road round to the right up to a T-junction. **Turn L**, signposted 'Newark, Mansfield', and at the next T-junction, **turn L**, signposted 'Mansfield' to Edingley. At the foot of the hill in Edingley, **turn R** into Station Road and about ½ mile later, **turn L** at a staggered crossroads, signposted 'Kirklington'. (This road crosses the Southwell Trail by an overbridge; if you want a short cut back to Southwell, **turn L** immediately after the bridge, then L on the Trail all the way back to Southwell.)

For the main route, continue to the next junction and **turn L**, signposted 'Kirklington', into Kirklington. At the junction with the A617 (which doesn't carry particularly heavy traffic), **turn L**, signposted 'Mansfield', and after about 500 yds, **turn R**, signposted 'Eakring'. This road climbs gently for about 1½ miles; at the brow of the hill a sign to the right points to the 'Duke's Wood Nature Reserve and Drilling Museum' – an unusual combination of a nature reserve and the site of what was Britain's largest inland oilfield.

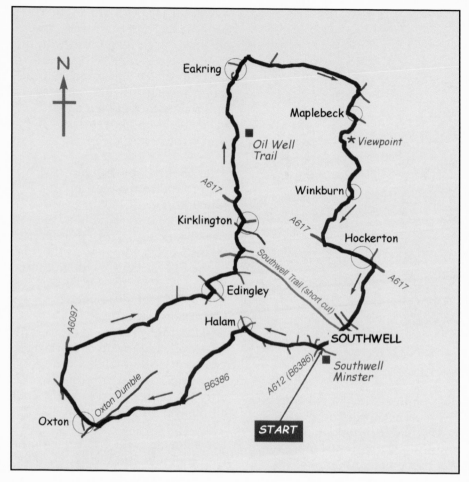

Continue down into Eakring and at the T-junction **turn R**, signposted 'Kneesall, Newark'. After about 2 miles, **turn R** at a staggered crossroads, signposted 'Maplebeck'. Follow this road as it **bears L** through the hamlet of Maplebeck. Towards the foot of the hill there is a pub on the left called The Beehive – claimed to be the smallest pub in Nottinghamshire (currently open lunchtime and evenings at weekends but evenings only during the week). Just beyond the pub, opposite the church, **turn R**, signposted 'Winkburn'.

The road climbs past Maplebeck Viewpoint, which has an orientation table and picnic area; on a clear day there are views right across to Lincoln Cathedral. In Winkburn, follow the road round to the right, signposted 'Kirklington, Hockerton, Newark'. At a T-junction with a main road (the A617) after about a mile, **turn L** (unsignposted). Some ¾ mile along this road, on the right, is the Hockerton Coffee Shop – which is also a fruit and veg shop, a bakery and delicatessen.

Continue into Hockerton and, just at the far end of the village, **turn R**, signposted 'Normanton, Southwell'. On the outskirts of Southwell, beside an imposing brick-built mill, now converted to flats, is the end of the Southwell Trail. Continue straight on over a crossroads to climb up beside the open green of the Burgage and then down to a mini-roundabout. **Turn L** into Church Street to return to the Minster car park.

• •

SOUTHWELL MINSTER

A cathedral in everything but name, Southwell Minster has been described as Nottinghamshire's finest, largest and most ancient church. Since 1884 it has been the cathedral church of the Diocese of Southwell. The present building was started in 1108 with many subsequent changes, including a doubling in size in the 1230s and 40s. The Minster's most prominent landmarks – the two pyramid-shaped 'pepperpot' steeples – date only from 1880 in their present form having been several times altered over earlier centuries. Now, with their light grey characteristic shape they show up from vantage points for some miles around the small and architecturally intriguing town, including the Maplebeck viewpoint on the later stages of the route. Southwell, by the way, is pronounced as the two distinct words 'South Well' by the people who live there and perversely as 'Suthell' by pretty well everybody else.

SOUTHWELL TRAIL

The Southwell Trail is one of several disused Nottinghamshire railway lines to find a new life as a path for walkers, horse-riders and cyclists. The surface is mostly firm gravel or ash but there are a few tree roots to keep a look out for. In summer the heavy hedgerows that have grown up beside it restrict the views rather, but it makes a pleasant off-road alternative. The best bit for cyclists is the section from near Farnsfield to Southwell – but look out for horses.

EAKRING AND THE OIL WELLS

A modest sign at the brow of the hill from Kirklington to Eakring points the way to one of Nottinghamshire's more unusual monuments: Britain's first onshore oilfield. The presence of oil was confirmed here in the late 1930s and the first well drilled in 1939. The oil was pumped to the surface by a series of up to 170 'nodding donkeys' – electric automatically-controlled beam pumps which nodded obediently when the oil level in the bore rose high enough. The Duke's Wood Trail now combines industrial archaeology with a nature trail dotted with restored nodding donkeys. (There are still two working nodding donkeys some 7 miles north of Eakring, near Bothamsall and quite close to Clumber Park, as well as others in Lincolnshire.) The site is now a haven for wildflowers and wildlife. There is a monument to American oil workers who in 1943 helped with the drilling and a small Visitor Centre at the site; you can get more information there (it's open most weekends) or from 01623 882446.

16

Newark's Northern Villages

26 or 13 miles

We have a confession to make: this route dips into Lincolnshire for a short way, partly to take in three or four pleasant villages but mainly to avoid having to use or make dogleg crossings of the busy A46 and A17 trunk roads. It's very easy terrain through woodland and open farming country: the highest point – about a couple of miles after the start – is not much more than 100 ft above sea level.

Map: OS Landranger 121 Lincoln and Newark-on-Trent.

Starting point: Newark Castle Station (GR 796543) (note: this is not the East Coast Main Line station – that is Newark Northgate – but the one on the Nottingham–Lincoln line). There is a car park nearby (not free) at the Waitrose supermarket and several others within a radius of a few hundred yards.

Short cuts: The route distance may be halved to about 13 miles by turning left instead of right after going through Stapleford Woods and then crossing the A46 north-east of Brough to join the A1133 south of Collingham. However, this short cut misses out almost all the villages.

Refreshments: There are several cafés and restaurants in Newark (a favourite, Gannets, opposite the Castle on Castle Gate, is open from 9.30 am to 4.30 pm on Sunday to Friday and 9 am to 5 pm on Saturday). There are pubs in Coddington, Thorpe on the Hill, Eagle, Collingham and Winthorpe. After Newark there appear to be no shops until Thorpe on the Hill, Eagle and Collingham.

The route: The terrain is pretty well flat: on this route the 85 ft 'summit' just before Collingham qualifies the nearby farm to be called Hill Farm and the 'hill' at Thorpe on the Hill is about the same! The roundabout crossing of the A17, between Coddington and Stapleford Woods, which you may prefer to cross on foot, a direct crossing of the busy A46 and just under a mile of the relatively quiet A1133 after Collingham are all the main road that is encountered on this route.

From Newark Castle Station, **turn L** on the B6326 (number not marked at this point) and go straight on over the River Trent, with Newark Castle on the right. At the roundabout by the Ossington Hotel, **turn L**, signposted 'Coddington', for about 200 yds to traffic lights by the White Swan. **Turn R**, signposted 'Coddington' again, and continue on this road (Queens Road which later becomes

Newark's refurbished waterfront

Sleaford Road) over the main railway line. At the traffic lights go straight on, now on Beacon Hill Road, over the A1 Newark bypass and through Coddington to a roundabout junction with the A17.

Go straight over, onto a minor road signposted 'Stapleford, Norton Disney'. This attractive road passes through the broad sweep of Stapleford Woods, a noted local beauty spot. After about 2 miles, soon after you come out of the woodland, **bear R** signposted 'Stapleford, Norton Disney' again. Go through Stapleford and, about a mile later at a junction where the road bears round to the right, **turn L** (effectively straight on) for about 300 yds.

On the outskirts of Norton Disney **turn R** (again effectively straight on), signed 'Clay Road – single track road'. After about 1½ miles **turn L** at a T-junction (effectively straight on) signposted 'Thurlby, Lincoln'. At another T-junction in Thurlby village after about ¾ mile **turn R**, signposted 'Haddington, Lincoln'. Carry straight on this road (it has some right-angle bends), ignoring the turn to Haddington village and following 'Thorpe on the Hill, Lincoln' signs. Go straight over the next crossroads into Haddington Lane, still signed 'Thorpe on the Hill, Lincoln'.

At the top of a slight slope a fine view of Lincoln Cathedral opens up to the right. In about another mile,

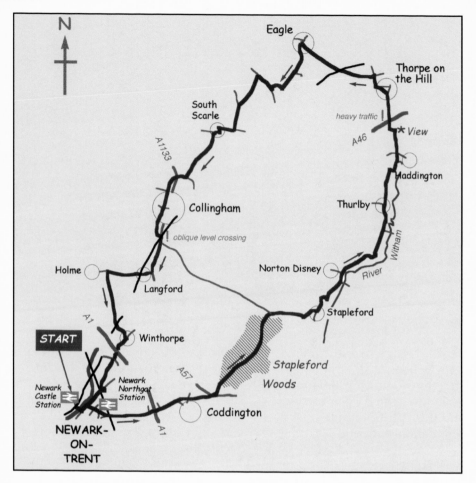

after a couple more right-angle bends you reach the A46. Cross the main road into another minor road, signposted 'Thorpe on the Hill, Doddington'.

In Thorpe on the Hill (the 'hill' reaches a dizzy 88 ft) **turn L** just in front of the very handsome church into Main Street, **bearing L and then R** on Station Road and downhill to a minor crossroads. **Turn L**, signposted 'Eagle', and

continue over the level crossing to Eagle village. After about 2 miles, in Eagle, **turn L** in front of the ornate archway that leads to the impressive church, signposted 'Eagle Hall, Morton, Swinderby', and about ½ mile later at a T-junction, **turn R**, signposted 'Eagle Hall, South Scarle, North Scarle'. At the next T-junction, at Eagle Hall, **turn R**, signposted 'North Scarle, South Scarle', and then take the **first L turning**, signposted 'South

Scarle'. After about a mile, soon after passing a wood to the left, **bear L** at a shallow T-junction, signed 'South Scarle, Newark', and then **R** at the next T-junction into South Scarle.

Follow the winding road through South Scarle and just at the end of the village, **turn L**, signposted 'Collingham, Newark'. About 1½ miles further on, on the outskirts of Collingham, **turn R** at a T-junction, still signposted 'Collingham, Newark'. Then, at the junction with the A1133 in Collingham, go straight over, into Low Street, signposted 'River Trent'. Shortly after, **bear R** at a green triangular island (effectively straight on) and soon after this **bear L** (again effectively straight on) into Cottage Lane.

Eventually, this lane turns sharp left to meet the A1133 by a level crossing. **Turn R** over the crossing. (Take care: the rails are oblique and it's best to make a sort of left-and-right wiggle so that you cross each rail as nearly as possible at right angles.) After about ¾ mile, take the **first turning on the R**, signposted 'Holme'. Continue for about a mile, over a level crossing, and as the village of Holme comes into view, **turn L** by a little brick bridge, signed 'Winthorpe, Newark'. After about 1½ miles, and another level crossing, you reach Winthorpe and **turn R** opposite a pub on a road signed 'Newark, footpath only'.

Follow this road to its end, then **bear R** to join a footpath which goes under the A1 and joins another short dead-end road. At the end of this road **bear R** onto a cycle path, signed 'Newark', which goes through an underpass under the A17, emerging into a residential road, Winthorpe Road. After about ¾ mile a cycle route is signposted to the right, 'Town Centre, Balderton'. Follow this along Hatchet's Lane and then under the B6166. The route keeps spiralling round to the left to climb to a cycle path parallel to the B6166.

Turn L over the railway to join the B6166. Go straight on at the traffic lights (you need to be in the right of the two lanes: if you're not confident about this, walk across when the way is clear). At the next roundabout by the Castle, **turn R**, signposted 'All other routes', and cross the river to get back to Newark Castle Station.

● ●

NEWARK-ON-TRENT
Newark has a wide range of architectural treasures – the Market Place is well worth a visit – while the aspect facing the River Trent is dominated by the Castle, which was founded around 1120.

STAPLEFORD WOODS
Stapleford Woods, a celebrated local beauty spot, is also a working forest composed mainly of conifers but with some broad-leaved trees. The woods are open to the public with a number of forest walks.

17

Lord Byron Country

26 or 13 miles

T his route meanders through a part of Nottinghamshire intimately associated with the poet Byron, who is buried in Hucknall church. Newstead Abbey was the family home, though when the poet inherited the title and the property, only the scullery was habitable! A small charge is payable to use the cycle route through the Abbey grounds. You then continue to Blidworth on a ridge road with broad views, and the second half of the figure-of-eight circuit takes you into Sherwood Pines Forest Park, with an opportunity to extend the ride (all off-road) to the Visitor Centre.

Maps: OS Landranger 129 Nottingham and Loughborough (but only for about ½ mile at the beginning and end of the route) and 120 Mansfield and Worksop.

Starting point: Hucknall railway station on the Robin Hood Line from Nottingham to Worksop (GR 540493). Hucknall is about 8 miles north-west of Nottingham city centre. There are height restriction barriers at the entrance and exit to the station car park.

Short cuts: The route distance may be halved to 13 miles by following the outward route to Blidworth and turning right into Field Lane to follow the return route back to Hucknall. This includes Newstead Abbey but not the fine woodland of Sherwood Pines Forest Park.

Refreshments: There is a tearoom at Newstead Abbey and another at the Visitor Centre in Sherwood Pines Forest Park. There are also pubs in all the villages on the route, and village shops in Blidworth, Bilsthorpe and Farnsfield.

The route: Unlike most of the rides which follow only roads, this one uses part of Route 6 of the 'National Cycle Network' ('NCN'), offering a helpful north-south link to Sherwood Pines Forest in an area without much alternative to A-roads. The route is mostly gently undulating, through a mix of farmland and forest, but there are a couple of quite appreciable climbs on the way back. As to main road, apart from about 300 yds of the A60 (surprisingly quiet at weekends) and just over a mile of the B6011 the roads carry very little traffic.

In Hucknall **turn L** out of the station, following the one-way system to the cross-roads by the Station Hotel. Go straight over for about a mile to a roundabout and on the far side join 'NCN' Route 6, through a barrier (awkward for tandems and trailers or trailer-

zag course through the residential village of Ravenshead, including a difficult sandy bridleway. An alternative if the A60 is quiet is to **turn L** on the main road for about 1½ miles, going straight ahead at the traffic lights after about 1¼ miles and then taking the **first turning R** (unsignposted) by a small wood. This attractive little ridge road with broad views south is soon joined again by Route 6.

At the next junction, after about 1¼ miles, where Route 6 is signed left, go straight on, still along the ridge with views opening up on both sides, to an oblique junction with the B6020, opposite Blidworth church. **Turn L** down the hill (exhilarating – but be careful!) and sweep round to the **L** at the bottom until Route 6 is once again signed to the right. **Turn R** and follow the Route 6 signs for nearly 3 miles; there are a couple of barriers but not nearly as difficult as the earlier ones, while the path is beautifully surfaced. It goes down a slope and **R** under a short tunnel, then climbs gently along the edge of some fine woodland.

At the second barrier, where the route meets a gravel forest road, **turn R** along the forest road (*see page 83); this eventually becomes a tarred road, reaching the A614 after about 2½ miles. Go straight across (care: the A614 can be busy) for about a mile to the centre of Bilsthorpe village. **Turn R** and ride through the straggling village for

In Hexgreave Park

bikes). The path climbs steadily in a shallow rock cutting with an abundance of wildflowers. At the second barrier go straight on until the path makes a dogleg right-and-left turn, bringing you out on the tarred road to Newstead Abbey.

Turn R (you may have to pay at the lodge, where there's a special much-reduced fee of 50p for people following the cycle route) and follow the road for 2 miles past the Abbey and its lakes and then climb steadily through rhododendron-fringed woodland to the exit onto the A60, opposite a pub called The Hutt. The 'official' Route 6 goes straight on here and follows a zig

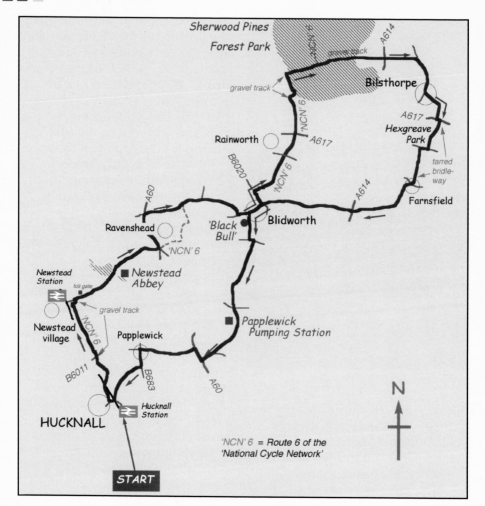

about another mile, then take the **L fork** (signposted 'Kirklington'), followed by an unsigned **R turn** after ½ mile to reach the A617.

Turn L for about 100 yds, then **R** by the lodge (use the small side gate if the main gate is shut). This pretty road is the private drive to Upper Hexgreave but – luckily for cyclists – has the status of a bridleway. There are two superb avenues; at the end of the second one **turn R** at the T-junction and **L** about 300 yds later into Farnsfield.

Turn R and **bear round to the L** after the church at a triangular green, along a winding road past the trim fields of a stud farm. A straight mile leads to the A614 again; cross – once more, with care – and carry on over the brow of the rise for about 2 miles to Blidworth. At the junction by the garage in Blidworth **turn L** up the hill you swooped down so joyfully on the way out and at the top **turn L** in front of the Black Bull inn into Field Lane.

Swoop down this straight open lane with a carefree heart – you don't have to go up it again – and **turn L** at the bottom, then **first R** (opposite the Horse and Groom) up a rise. This is merely a prelude to the day's real climb, up a delightful road, mixed forest to the left and with meadows full of horses to the right. Once over the top the road drops steadily to a crossroads. Go straight over to pass the prominent local landmark of Papplewick Pumping Station, with its tall chimney and ornate gateway. When you reach a T-junction, **turn R** (effectively straight on) to the traffic lights on the A60.

Turn R at the lights and continue for about 300 yds, **then L** on the B6011 (signposted 'Hucknall'). This climbs slightly for a short distance then swoops down between open fields to Papplewick village. At the crossroads by the Griffin's Head, **turn L** on the B683 (signposted 'Hucknall'), then **R** after about 500 yds into Papplewick Lane (still signposted 'Hucknall'). This road brings you back to Hucknall Station.

• • • • • • • • • • • • • • • • • • •

THE BYRON CONNECTION

Although the 6th Lord Byron lived only to the age of 36 and spent his last nine years abroad, he is widely commemorated hereabouts – the local cinema and bingo hall is even called 'The Byron', as are a pub and numerous businesses. The family had a history of financial problems and the ancestral home, Newstead Abbey, which incorporates the remains of an earlier priory, fell into disrepair. Byron managed to extend the habitable area but, like his forebears, he too was soon in debt. Following rumours and scandal he settled abroad where he wrote his best work, and then joined the struggle for Greek independence from Turkish rule only to die of malaria in 1824. He is buried in the family vault in Hucknall church. The Abbey and its grounds now belong to the City of Nottingham. Telephone 01623 455900 for further details.

SHERWOOD PINES FOREST PARK

Just to the north of the northern part of this route, Forest Enterprise has opened up to the public as a Forest Park a network of paths and tracks within the former Clipstone Forest. These include two waymarked cycle trails which lead to the Sherwood Pines Visitor Centre with its tearoom and open picnic area. To join them from the point marked * in the route description, follow the Route 6 signs across an open level crossing about ¼ mile after the barrier until you reach a wide forest road, then turn right and follow the wooden waymarkers with blue and green cycle symbols. Going to the Visitor Centre and back adds about 6 (all off-road) miles to the total distance.

PAPPLEWICK PUMPING STATION

Papplewick Pumping Station was one of several ringing Nottingham, built around 1880 to supply water to the city. The Papplewick station has a steam-powered beam pumping engine which operates on some Sundays and bank holidays, and is housed in an elaborate Victorian building.

18

On the Trail of D. H. Lawrence

13 miles

We tried in vain to find an elegant circular route which would take in places with D. H. Lawrence connections and still avoid the narrow and rather busy A608, so this route is in three loops with an optional out-and-home detour to the D. H. Lawrence Birthplace Museum and Durban House Heritage Centre. Since Lawrence's day, around the start of the 20th century, there has been a great deal of new building in these parts, quite a bit of it connected with coalmines which came, flourished and died in the years between. Nevertheless, enough of the open countryside remains much in the state it was when young 'Bert Lawrence' travelled over it as a boy and young man.

Maps: OS Landranger 129 Nottingham and Loughborough and 120 Mansfield and Worksop.

Starting point: Colliers Wood Wildlife Reserve car park (GR 481481) – height barrier at the entrance, so watch it if you've got bikes on a roof rack. Langley Mill Station, served by (some) Midland Mainline and Central Trains services from Nottingham, Chesterfield and Sheffield, is about 2 miles west of the start. The Reserve is about 9 miles north-west of Nottingham, just off the B600.

Short cuts: Since the route is in three loops it can be easily shortened by cutting out any one or two of them.

Refreshments: There is a wide choice of cafés and pubs and shops in Eastwood (including a café/restaurant almost opposite the Birthplace Museum), and the route passes Minton's Tearoom next to Greasley church. There are pubs in Underwood, Bagthorpe, Moorgreen, and Beauvale.

The route: The terrain is quite up-and-down, with a tough little climb out of Bagthorpe. The rewards are some extensive and unexpected views towards Matlock and the Derbyshire foothills of the Peak District. The route is mostly on-road with about 1½ miles of firm bridleway down to Moorgreen Reservoir. There is a very short (150 yd) section of A-road: the A608 just before Underwood.

From the Colliers Wood car park **turn R** (no signpost) to a T-junction with the B600 (signed at this point just as Moorgreen – otherwise there's no sign). **Turn L** and follow this road for nearly 2 miles to Underwood. Very shortly after the A608 comes in from the left and just after the sign for Underwood, **turn L** on the prominently signed Main Road (otherwise unsignposted, except to the Hole in the Wall pub). At the far end of the village just before the road begins to go downhill there's an open space to the left, Underwood Hill, with an orientation table showing what Peak District landmarks you can see from here.

Around halfway down the hill, just when there's a temptation to let the bike go, there is a small cross-roads. **Turn R** into Wansley Lane, signposted 'Lower Bagthorpe'. (Partway down to here there's a road which goes to the intriguingly named 'Plain Spot'; you can go round that loop if you like to see if it's true (it is). Since the route also goes to Bogend we were tempted by 'Plain Spot to Bogend' as a title.)

Towards the end of Bagthorpe village, opposite a pub called Dixies Arms, **turn R** up Church Lane (no signpost). This is quite a tough little climb up. When Underwood church spire is clearly in sight about 200 yds ahead but before the top of the hill, **turn L** on a completely unsigned bridleway immediately before a white house, No 100. At the end of the bridleway go straight over by the Victorian Posy Shop (signposted 'Mansfield, M1' though you can't see the sign from here) to a crossroads with the A608 by the Sandhills Tavern. Go straight on down the delightful Felley Mill Lane North (no signpost) until you come to a vehicle barrier at the end of the tarred road.

This is the site of the former Felley Mill. Carry on for a few yards along this track and take the **third path off to the R** where a prominent bridleway goes off to the left. There's a short and quite stiff little climb after which this very attractive path rolls through woodland with first a stream and then Moorgreen Reservoir to the right. For the most part it is firm-surfaced and very easily ridable on any sort of bike, though there is the occasional little gully (probably seasonal) where small streams come down from the left. Eventually the path reaches a tarred road, where you **bear slightly R** to the junction with the B600.

Turn L, opposite a sign reading 'Moorgreen' once again (there is also a D. H. Lawrence information board 'The country of my heart', at this junction). After about ¾ mile, at the top of a slight hill and just past the Horse and Groom, **turn L**, signposted 'New Road' leading to Narrow Road. In about a mile – through archetypal D. H. Lawrence country – you can just see all that's left of Beauvale Priory to the left: merely fragments of a window and wall incorporated into a farm building, and not open to the public. The road climbs to reach Brookbreasting Farm, where the road becomes Narrow Lane, though there's no sign to mark the change.

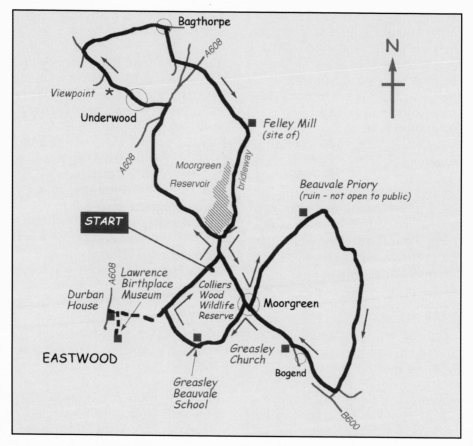

Continue along the lane for another 1½ miles to the junction with the B6009.

Turn R (effectively straight on) and **then R again** after about 100 yds – before the T-junction with the B600 – into Church Road and down past the few houses of picturesquely named Bog End. At the junction with the B600 **turn R** (no sign). After about ½ mile, opposite the Horse and Groom, **turn L** into Moorgreen, signposted 'Newthorpe, Eastwood, D. H. Lawrence

Birthplace'. Continue for about ¾ mile, then, about 100 yds past the Ram Inn on the right, **turn R** at the Greasley Beauvale D. H. Lawrence Infant School into Mill Road, signposted 'Lower Beauvale'. At the foot of the hill, **turn R** opposite a house named Brook Hill (no signpost) to go back to the starting point.

*To visit the D. H. Lawrence Birthplace Museum and the Durban House Heritage Centre (a detour of just under 2 miles there and back), **turn L** at the foot of Mill Road. Where this*

road meets the A608 the Durban House Heritage Centre is on the left. To visit the D. H. Lawrence Birthplace Museum without climbing up the main road, take the **last turning on the L** before the main road (just after a children's playground sign), Moorfields Avenue. At the end of this dead-end road, turn L and walk along a narrow footpath which emerges onto another road, Grange View (though there's no sign here). **Turn R** on the road and look out for another footpath on the L, between Nos 33 and 35, which cuts through to the next road up. Opposite is Albert Street. Go up this road, then **turn R** to walk along the restored street of miners' houses to the Museum which is on Victoria Street. On the return, the path back down to Moorfields Avenue is just before a bungalow, No 18.

• •

THE LAWRENCE CONNECTION

David Herbert Lawrence was born in Eastwood in 1885, the son of a miner, and was educated at the school in Greasley which now bears his name. He went on to be the first local boy to go to the then University College at Nottingham. Many local settings are used for his novels and short stories, sometimes under their own names but more often thinly disguised, sometimes with different names in different works. Of those on our route, Felley Mill becomes 'Strelley Mill' and Beauvale

Priory 'The Abbey' in *The White Peacock*, and the church at Greasley is 'Greymede Church' in *The White Peacock*, 'Minton Church' in *Sons and Lovers*, and appears under its own name in several of the short stories. Moorgreen Reservoir is 'Nethermere' in *The White Peacock* and 'Willey Water' in *Women in Love*. Several of the stretches of countryside that our route passes, remain much as Lawrence knew them (though, ironically, less industrial now than then) and it is easy to recognise the country round Moorgreen and Bagthorpe from his evocative descriptions. In Eastwood, Lawrence's birthplace is preserved as a museum and Durban House ½ mile away with its long coalmining associations is now the Durban House Heritage Centre. It and the D. H. Lawrence Birthplace Museum are open every day of the week from 10 am to 5 pm in April to October, and from 10 am to 4 pm in November to March. They are closed from Christmas Eve to New Year's Day. Tel. 01773 717353.

BAGTHORPE

Almost hidden in its little valley, Bagthorpe is largely a remnant of pre-industrial Nottinghamshire. With its stream, copses and farms, this is how the countryside looked before the pits came and went. In those days the village was by comparison a good deal larger than many of its neighbours and had an influence well beyond its boundaries. Indeed, one of Nottingham's large hospitals can trace its origins back to a local charity and Bagthorpe workhouse. Now largely a dormitory village it retains its peace and tranquillity. But it's a steep-sided little valley to climb out of!

19

Vale of Belvoir

26 miles

The Vale of Belvoir (pronounced 'Beever') stretches away east into Lincolnshire, and this route leads into the Nottinghamshire end of it. This is archetypical rural Middle England, bounded to the south by the ridge that culminates in Belvoir Castle. The Vale is peppered with small intimate villages, some picturesque, others more workmanlike. There are points on this route where, looking out across the trim fields, copses and hedgerows, you can see as many as half-a-dozen church spires rising above the trees. The River Trent has always been a natural barrier and the now-quiet villages along the river on the first part of the route saw some hard-fought skirmishes during the English Civil War in the 1640s as both sides tried to maintain their control of the river crossings.

Map: OS Landranger 129 Nottingham and Loughborough.

Starting point: Radcliffe on Trent centre (GR 646393); there is a free car park almost opposite the centre, south of Main Road, off Richmond Terrace. Fairly infrequent trains run from Nottingham and Grantham (Central Trains) to Radcliffe Station (about 300 yds along the route from the centre of Radcliffe). For several services it is a 'request stop' – you tell the conductor if you want to get off at Radcliffe, or hail it like a bus if you want to board it there. Radcliffe on Trent is about 5 miles east of Nottingham. An alternative would be to ride from Nottingham Midland Station via Adbolton (see map).

Short cuts: The route could be shortened by going straight from Flintham to Car Colston but that misses the Scarrington horseshoes.

Refreshments: There is a café in Radcliffe on Trent but it's not always open at weekends, and pubs in Radcliffe, Shelford, Gunthorpe (just off the route, across the Trent at Gunthorpe Bridge), East Bridgford, Flintham, Screveton (about 200 yards off the route) and Car Colston. There are village shops in Radcliffe-on-Trent and East Bridgford.

The route: The terrain is gentle for most of the route, except for quite a steep little pitch up from the River Trent after crossing the A6097, and the easier climb out of East Bridgford. There are two dogleg crossings of the A46 Fosse Way which involve about 200 and 400 yds of this busy main road, and two simpler straight-over crossings of the A6097.

The horseshoe stack at Scarrington

From the centre of Radcliffe on Trent, turn north-east (**L** if you're coming from Nottingham) by the Co-op Late Shop, signposted 'Shelford, East Bridgford', and continue for about 2½ miles to climb over the brow of Malkin Hill, which offers broad views to the left over the River Trent in its valley. The road then drops to a crossroads; **turn L**, signposted 'Shelford', **bearing R** at the foot of the hill to wind through the village of Shelford, then alongside the River Trent.

About 2 miles beyond Shelford there is a crossroads with the A6097 by Gunthorpe Bridge. Go straight over, signposted 'East Bridgford', first beside the river then uphill into East Bridgford. At the crossroads by the church, **turn L** into Kneeton Road, signposted 'Kneeton'. The road climbs gently, past a converted windmill; at a T-junction after about 2 miles, **turn R**, signposted 'Newark, Nottingham', continuing for about a mile to a T-junction with the A46, on the line of the Roman Fosse Way.

Turn R on the A46 (care!), signposted 'Leicester', and after about 200 yds, **L** at Red Lodge Antiques (a former pub), signposted 'Screveton'. (It would be possible to walk along the grass verge to this corner if you don't want to ride on the A46 which at times carries quite heavy traffic.) At a T-junction at the end of this road, in Screveton, opposite a phone box, **turn L** (unsigned) and then after about 200 yds, go straight on, signed 'Flintham, Newark'.

After 1½ miles, at the T-junction in Flintham, **turn R**, signposted 'Sibthorpe, Hawksworth', past the Boot and Shoe Inn. In about 1 mile, **turn L** on a minor road, signposted 'Sibthorpe', and follow this road round to the right into the hamlet of Sibthorpe. **Turn R**, signposted 'Hawksworth, Scarrington', through Top Green to a minor crossroads. **Turn L**, signposted 'Thoroton, Aslockton', then after another ¾ mile, at the next crossroads, **turn R**, again signposted 'Thoroton, Aslockton'.

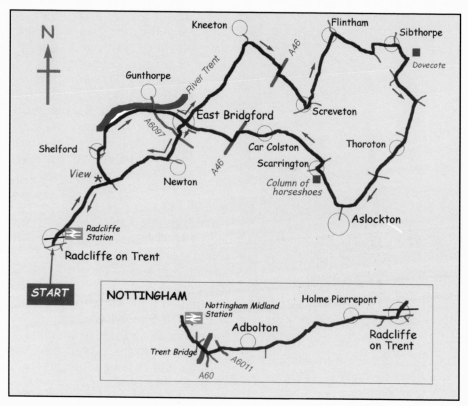

Go straight on through Thoroton, ignoring all right and left turns, until you reach the outskirts of Aslockton. Take the **first R turning**, signposted 'Scarrington', to pass the column of used horseshoes at the entry to Scarrington. At the church shortly afterwards, **turn R**, signposted 'Hawksworth, Sibthorpe', then the **first L**, signed 'Car Colston'. Car Colston is noted for its two big village greens and the road crosses the Large Green to reach the A46 at a T-junction.

Turn L, signed 'Leicester', and then, after about 400 yds, **turn R**, signposted 'East Bridgford'. (Once again there is a grass verge if you don't want to ride along the A46, and a central refuge at the junction which aids crossing.) The crossroads by the church at the centre of East Bridgford is about 1½ miles down this road; at the crossroads, **turn L**, signposted 'Newark, Radcliffe'. After about ¼ mile the route reaches the A6097 at a light-controlled crossroads and you go straight over, signed 'Newton, RAF Newton', and continue for about ¾ mile to a T-junction. **Turn R**, signposted 'Shelford, Radcliffe', and follow this road the 4 miles or so back to Radcliffe on Trent.

Link routes from and to Nottingham Midland Station

Link from Nottingham: **Turn L** outside the station and follow the bus-and-cycle lane straight on at the first light-controlled junction into Arkwright Street, with the Queen's Hotel on the right. Go straight over at the next light-controlled junction and almost immediately bear right opposite Carpetmania on a pedestrian-and-cycle underpass into a paved path that leads to The Meadows Bridgeway Shopping Centre. **Turn L** by the Poet's Corner pub, following the blue cycle route sign 'Trent Bridge, West Bridgford'. After a short distance **turn R** into Arkwright Walk, at a fingerpost signed 'Trent Bridge, St Saviour's Church', with cycle symbols on the ground. At the end of Arkwright Walk at the junction with Radcliffe Street go effectively straight on, following cycle signs for 'Trent Bridge, Embankment', leaving the carriageway along a red-surfaced cycle path across Bathley Street to pass between Boots Social Club to the right and Topknot Hair and Beauty to the left, then cross an unsigned road via the central refuge. You are now at the north side of Trent Bridge. Walk across the dual carriageway via the pedestrian crossing, then **turn R** over the bridge. On the south side of the river **turn L** into Radcliffe Road at a light-controlled junction, signed 'Nottingham, Radcliffe, National Water Sports Centre'.

After about 500 yds go straight over at the next light-controlled junction into Trent Boulevard, signed 'Lady Bay area only', avoiding the left fork into Holme Road. The built-up area stops quite abruptly after about a mile, and after a further 500 yds, **turn L** at the T-junction with Adbolton Lane, to pass the National Watersports Centre. Continue straight on past a 'no through road' sign, then along a short untarred and potholed section of road (care!), just past the entrance to the imposing brick-built Holme Pierrepont Hall. Continue to a T-junction opposite Camelot Garage, then **turn L** past the church and the Manvers Arms to the centre of Radcliffe on Trent.

Return link to Nottingham: At the T-junction by the Co-op Late Shop, turn right, signposted 'Nottingham', and just after the Cliff Inn turn right into The Green. Retrace the outgoing route past the National Water Sports Centre and take the first turn right after the campsite, into Adbolton Lane, by Skylarks Nursing Home. Follow this road, which becomes Trent Boulevard*, for about 1½ miles to a light-controlled junction. Go straight over (bearing slightly right), signposted 'Trent Bridge', and at the next light-controlled junction follow straight-on signs (effectively right) to cross Trent Bridge. (This is quite a busy and involved junction and you may find it easier to use the pedestrian crossing to reach the west side of the road, then walk across Trent Bridge by the pavement to reach the cycle route.) If you are on the road, stay in the left-lane marked 'Buses and Meadows only' and follow the road as it it bears round to the left, passing a sign 'no entry except buses and cycles', then at the signalled junction by Carpetmania go straight on to the station.

*As an alternative, there are a couple of points on Trent Boulevard where a cycle route is signed to the right. This leads by the riverside path and the suspension bridge back to the station: just follow the cycle signs for 'City Centre' – as Route 20 – to pass the station.

● ●

SHELFORD
Shelford – 'the place of the shallow ford' – is now scarcely larger than at the time of the Domesday Book: both modern and 11th-century censuses put the population at around 250. Shelford nestles in a curve of the Trent and is very picturesque seen from the crossroads on the route above the village with the river and hills to the north as a backdrop. The shallow ford was eventually replaced by a pedestrian ferry to Stoke Bardolph on the left bank which ran until the 1970s. The gentle pace of Shelford life is perhaps exemplified by the fact that the ferry is still signposted from the village. But it was not always so: there were some very bloody skirmishes along this part of the Trent valley in the Civil War and few worse than the slaughter of about 200 besieged Royalists at Shelford Manor.

THE SCARRINGTON HORSESHOES
One of the most striking features here is a 17 ft high column of some 50,000 used horseshoes, beside the Aslockton road. For all its historic look, the stack is in fact quite recent, having been accumulated by the local smith in the twenty years leading up to his retirement in 1965. When there was a threat that this local landmark might be sold to America, the local authority stepped in and the pile now belongs to Nottinghamshire County Council.

20

Nottinghamshire Wolds

26 miles

The pleasure of a route like this is in the actual travel, on quiet roads through the countryside, rather than an abundance of specific 'places of interest', and despite its city centre start this is a very rural route, with a mixture of pasture, arable land and broad-leafed woodland. Don't forget that 'wolds' are hills, so the southern part has one or two quite hilly sections – though the climbs are short.

Map: OS Landranger 129 Nottingham and Loughborough.

Starting point: Nottingham Midland Station (GR 575393). There is a pay-and-display car park at the station and several others nearby. Some have height restrictions.

Short cuts: There are several opportunities for shortening the route, the most obvious by going straight from Wysall through Widmerpool to Kinoulton.

Refreshments: There are cafés in Ruddington, soon after the start, and Cotgrave, towards the end; neither is open on a Sunday. There are also pubs in all the villages on the route except Owthorpe. There is a village shop at Willoughby-on-the-Wolds. The canal basin in Hickling makes an attractive picnic spot, with the possibility of a stroll along the canal towpath.

The route: From Bradmore to just after Upper Broughton and from Owthorpe to Cotgrave the terrain is rolling with one or two quite stiff but fairly short climbs; fortunately, you go down the steepest and longest hill, into Cotgrave. Otherwise it is fairly flat. There are three short stretches of A-road; two are not very busy and the other has a separate cycle and pedestrian path. Take care crossing the fast A52 towards the end of the route.

From Nottingham Midland Station, cross the street in front of the station, Carrington Street (cycle gap in the central reservation), following the blue cycle sign 'Meadows, Wilford, Clifton' to join the prominent red-surfaced cycle path. Continue southwards along this path, crossing three sets of light-controlled crossings to join the wide tree-lined and traffic-free Queens Walk. Continue along this to the roundabout and its end, and then follow cycle route signs to 'Wilford, Clifton' over Wilford Toll Bridge (cycle and pedestrian only), then continue straight on along a minor road through Wilford village to a light-controlled junction with Wilford Lane.

Go straight over (slight **R and L**) into Ruddington Lane and follow this road for about 2 miles to Ruddington. At the crossroads by the Bricklayer's Arms, **turn L** into Kirk Lane, signposted 'Nottingham, Loughborough, A60'. After about 400 yds, at a light-controlled crossroads, **turn R** on the A60, signposted 'Loughborough'. Go straight over the next roundabout, past Bradmore village and at the end of the village take the **second turn L**, Pendock Lane, signposted 'Keyworth, Wysall'.

Continue on this road for about 2½ miles, following signs for 'Wysall' – there's quite a stiff little hill about halfway along. At a T-junction on the outskirts of Wysall, **turn R** on Keyworth Road, signposted 'Widmerpool, Wymeswold' and continue down the hill as far as the Plough Inn. **Turn L** after the pub, signposted 'Widmerpool, Willoughby, Foss Road'. After about ½ mile, take the **first turn R** (dilapidated signpost with no arms at the time we checked) and continue for about 2 miles to Willoughby-on-the-Wolds. Take the **first turn L**, Main Street, signposted 'Upper Broughton, Widmerpool', and continue through the village past the church and the Three Horseshoes. The road bears round to the right to a T-junction.

Turn L, signposted 'Upper Broughton, Melton Mowbray', to cross over the A46 and follow signs for 'Upper Broughton' for about 2½ miles. At a fork by a green on the outskirts of Upper Broughton, **turn L** into Top Green, **keeping L** at another fork, to meet the A606. **Turn L** up the quite steep hill for about 250 yds and then just before the brow **turn R** into Hickling Lane, an unsignposted minor road; this is a slightly tricky junction on a bend and you might find it easier to walk across although the A606 isn't particularly busy on this stretch. After about a mile, at the far end of an unfenced stretch, **turn R** at an unsigned T-junction, and then after about 300 yds, **turn L** at another T-junction, signposted 'Hickling, Kinoulton'.

Go through Hickling and Kinoulton, following signs for 'Owthorpe'. Soon after passing the prominent poplar avenue to Vimy Ridge Farm on the left (consult the tourist information board by the avenue), **turn L** (effectively straight on), signposted 'Owthorpe'. At a crossroads with the dead-end road to the hamlet of Owthorpe ahead, **turn L**, signposted 'Nottingham, Newark', to go up Owthorpe Hill. Go straight over (care!) at the crossroads with the A46, signposted 'Cotgrave', and go over the brow and then down the hill into Cotgrave.

At the foot of the hill continue straight on to a T-junction; **turn R**,

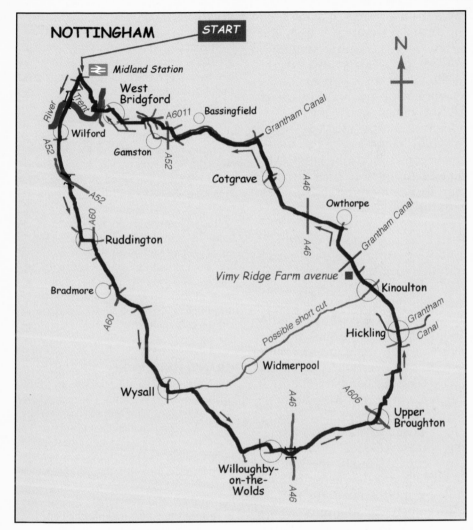

NOTTINGHAM **START**

Midland Station

West Bridgford

Bassingfield

A6011

River Trent

Wilford

A52

Gamston

A52

Grantham Canal

Cotgrave

A46

Owthorpe

Grantham Canal

A46

A60

Ruddington

Vimy Ridge Farm avenue

Kinoulton

Bradmore

A60

Possible short cut

Hickling

Grantham Canal

Widmerpool

Wysall

A46

A606

Upper Broughton

Willoughby-on-the-Wolds

A46

N

signposted 'Nottingham', to pass the church on the left to another T-junction. **Turn L** and continue for about a mile to the point where the road crosses the Grantham Canal. **Turn L** immediately before the canal onto the towpath, which has a firm compacted stone surface. Follow this for about 2 miles until it reaches a minor road. **Turn R** (no sign) and about 100 yds later, before reaching the main road, **turn R** into Bassingfield Lane, signposted 'Bassingfield'. After about 250 yds, where the road bears round to the right and just before the Bassingfield village sign, **turn L** on an unsigned path between some concrete bollards down to the A52.

Cross the main road, making use of the central reservation (care!), and on the far side continue straight on to reach a minor road. Go straight on along this road, past a telephone box and an old signpost for Nottingham and West Bridgford; shortly after this the road bears sharply round to the left and becomes Kirkstone Drive. At the next T-junction, **turn R** (no sign) to a light-controlled junction with the A6011.

Turn L onto a signed cycle-and-pedestrian path to cross the canal and then **turn L** into Davies Road. Take the **first L**, Brockley Road, and then the **first R**, Blake Road and follow this to the centre of West Bridgford. **Turn R** through the centre of West Bridgford to a minor roundabout. Go straight on along Central Avenue, and straight on at the next minor roundabout on Bridgford Road. After about 400 yds, opposite a park, follow a blue-and-white cycle sign 'Meadows, City Centre' to the **L**, into Millicent Road. Follow the cycle route signs, crossing London Road, the A60, at a 'sheep-pen' crossing into Sandringham Road then along the river bank to cross the Trent by the suspension cycle and pedestrian bridge. Once across the bridge, **turn R** on the road past the Memorial Park, then follow the blue signs for the city centre. The cycle route passes Nottingham Midland Station.

RUDDINGTON

Ruddington was one of a number of Nottinghamshire villages at the centre of the hosiery trade in the 19th century. Frame-knitters' cottages are characterised by long windows, often on opposite sides of the room used as a workshop. In the days when oil and candles were the only sources of artificial light, these broad windows made the best of the available daylight. There are two of these cottages in Ruddington, furnished as they would have been in 1850 and 1900, but the main part of the Ruddington Framework Knitters Museum (open Tuesday to Saturday from April to December, plus bank holiday Mondays) is housed in what was a larger workshop with room for 50 frames. The museum now has about 25, most of them in working order. Ruddington also has a Village Museum, chronicling the history of everyday life in the village.

GRANTHAM CANAL

The Grantham Canal originally ran – not surprisingly – to Grantham from the River Trent at Nottingham and was opened in 1797. It carried commercial traffic for 132 years, eventually closing in 1929. Over the following decades humpback bridges were levelled into culverts and relatively recently roadbuilding has severed the Nottingham end. Now there are moves to restore the canal, including a very ambitious plan to reopen it to navigation. Locks which had been concreted in are being reopened and, more important from a cyclist's point of view, the towpath has been restored with a firm surface.